GENDER GOGGLES

THE VISION YOU NEED TO GET PROMOTED, STRENGTHEN RELATIONSHIPS & LOVE GRACIOUSLY

JILL EATON

ISBN: 979-8-6863418-6-9

First Edition: October 2020

Table of Contents

INTRODUCTION

There are many reasons why someone opens a book about gender. You may just be curious or had an experience that left you wondering, or you may be skeptical that there are any gender differences at all. If you are like most people, you're at least wondering if it is helpful to talk about this. Doesn't talking about gender differences drive more division between us?

Gender communication is a topic that most people aren't comfortable talking about. I titled this book *Gender Goggles* because everyone sees gender through their own lens, experience, and filters. Our relationships benefit from observing things from a broader viewpoint or set of "goggles."

I must be clear that there is a spectrum of behavior for all human beings. On one end, we have behaviors traditionally categorized as feminine, while on the other end, we see masculine behaviors. For clarity's sake, I will be pointing out the behaviors closer to the ends of the spectrum, but please keep in mind that we are all at different places on the spectrum based on many factors.

For example, my behaviors would be considered more on the male end of the spectrum even though I identify as a female both in sex and gender. My closest sibling is a male, and I played competitive athletics in school, worked in computer science, and spent three decades in a male-dominated technical field. All of this contributed to my place on the spectrum for communication. Each individual is unique.

Early in my career, I was a leader in the company women's affinity group, and each leader was challenged to come up with a topic to share with other women. I created a presentation to teach women how to communicate better in the workplace. While researching, I discovered fascinating information regarding how gender affects peoples' communication styles. Deborah Tannen's bestseller *Talking from 9 to 5: Women and Men at Work* paved the way for researchers like me to dig in on the different ways men and women communicate. It felt as if a filter had been removed from my eyes, and I started to see things from a different perspective.

Everywhere I went, I studied people, making mental notes of my observations—how people stood, how they interacted in business meetings, and how they behaved at parties. I devoured books on the topic and stayed informed as research revealed new insights. I implemented all that I discovered into presentations, opening others' eyes as mine had been opened. The presentations were well received, and it wasn't long before I presented to much broader audiences. There was one particularly memorable presentation.

I sat in my office when someone rapped on the door. A man I didn't recognize poked his head around the door, a polite smile on his face.

"Do you remember me?" he asked. Scrolling through my mental contact list as quickly as possible, I couldn't place him anywhere. I had no idea who he was.

"I'm so sorry, but I don't. How may I help you?" I hoped that he wouldn't be offended at my memory lag, but he didn't seem to mind.

"I was at the presentation that you gave on gender differences in India three years ago. Do you remember the presentation?"

I'm sure my eyebrows met my hairline because I remembered it as one of the worst presentations I ever gave. I'd traveled to India on a business trip and presented the gender communication differences information to an IT leadership team. Their organization had been working to increase their gender diversity and had applied to be an Employer of Choice for Women— they were serious about making the changes necessary to make sure that all their leaders learned to communicate with their employees regardless of gender.

At the time, the entire leadership team was male, and their body language screamed that they were uncomfortable and did not want to be there. I gave my usual presentation to the most non-responsive and subdued audience I had ever experienced. A cricket chirping would've been a welcome response. No one had any questions at the end. No reactions. No nods. No nothing. We were all ready to leave the room as quickly as possible!

Afterward, I chalked it up to jet lag and tried to make sure my next presentation was better.

Now, looking at the face of one of the audience members of what I considered to be my worst presentation, my smile must have cracked. I forced a laugh, "Yes, I remember that it didn't go over very well!"

To my surprise, he disagreed with me entirely.

"Oh no, what you said shocked us, and we were unsure of the appropriate way to express it." Before I could gather a response, he continued, "I have come here to your office to thank you. You do not know it, but your presentation that day saved my marriage. We were struggling, and I blamed her until I heard your presentation. I understood that the issues we were experiencing were because of the differences you mentioned."

This small interaction changed my life. I realized that understanding how gender differences affect communication can significantly impact others' lives, just as it impacted my own. That is why I wrote this book and am sharing the research, stories, advice, and examples from my own life to help you see new perspectives on the impact of gender communications.

I hope you'll join the countless number of people I've worked with over the last fifteen years who now understand how to communicate more effectively.

1

FOUNDATIONAL CONCEPTS

Impact of Childhood Games

Being a modern and forward-thinking young mother, I bought my eldest a vast array of gender-neutral toys. Stephanie played with Legos, puzzles, barbie dolls, books, a microscope, nerf balls, sports equipment, stuffed animals, computer games, etc. Jeremy, born four years later, inherited the same set of toys. Despite my determination that my children's play would not be bound by their sex, I was continually shocked to see the differences between their use of toys. Stephanie and her buddies jumped one or two at a time on our trampoline, singing or telling stories while jumping. Jeremy and his friends reenacted World Wrestling and would not stop until someone bled or night fell—whichever came first.

To fully understand the differences in the way boys and girls interact with their friends, we must understand the difference between play and games and how they shape our communication styles.

Play tends to be unstructured. It's informal with no rules, scorekeeping, or defined end goal. Meanwhile, games have a winner and a loser. Games have rules, and there is a clear end goal.

The way we communicate and interact with people around us develops in early childhood. A study of children's playground games showed that boys tend to participate in games with a winner and loser and in groups of three or more (Pellegrini, Kato, Blatchford, & Baines, 2002). As a result, boys end up with more experience navigating a structural hierarchy, competition, aggressiveness, and learn to set aside their emotions to focus on the end goal. Boys are taught not to question the coach/leader in public. In boys' games, they will often have some of their friends on the opposing team, and they will be on the same team with people they dislike. They learn to resolve disputes on the playing field and resume their friendships once the game is finished.

Conversely, girls typically participate in play that is role-playing or relationship-based with one or two other girls. Typical girls' play provides them more experience interacting with others, talking, sharing feelings, and taking turns. The relationships continue even when the play activity is completed. This key distinction helps us better understand gender communication differences in adults, too.

It's important to note that, although this is typical for male/female play, communication is never one-size-fits-all. For example, I have four older sisters, but I grew up playing with my brother the most because he was the next closest in age. Following him around the countryside by our house, I often wound up playing basketball, riding ATVs, playing cards, Monopoly, fishing, and shooting bow and arrows. Once, we found a newly dead raccoon and dissected it to see what its brain looked like (it was a very cool, slightly gross, experiment)! Needless to say, I did not grow up engaging in typical female play, which often left me at a loss when making friends as I entered adolescence.

Girls I tried to befriend typically wanted to play role-play types of games. However, due to my experiences with play during my formative years, I never really liked those games. Instead, I'd always reach for board games or puzzles when playing with others. Although I am a woman and do have many traits on the female end of the spectrum, there are some I don't have because of the socialization I experienced as a child. This is normal despite my conditioning being less common for girls— it's the nature/nurture argument come to life. We all fall on various points on the spectrum, and where I fall sometimes puts me on slightly different footing than my female peers.

In the June 2010, *Scientific American Mind* article "He Said, She Said," Deborah Tannen describes an example from her research that shows videos of four boys at a daycare center discussing how high they can hit a ball. The first boy raises his arm above his head and says, "Mine is up to there!" then each boy brags about how much higher they can hit the ball than the previous boy, with the fourth boy finally declaring, "Mine's all the way up to God!"

She contrasts those videos to one of two girls who use similitude to create bonds with each other—even at the expense of correctness. The first girl looks at the second and says, "Did you know my babysitter, called Amber, has already contacts?" The second girl replies gleefully, "My mom has already contacts, and my dad does too!" The first girl then pauses and delightfully exclaims, "The same!"

The second girl matched the observation about contacts and used the same incorrect grammar, forming a connection via creating bonds of similarity. The article concludes that sameness brings similar joy to the girls as topping one another does for the boys because, although men and women have different *styles* of communication, they have the same *goals*. We all aspire to be powerful, and we all want to connect with others. Our position on the gender spectrum may help us identify if we need to adapt our behavior to achieve those goals.

Hierarchy and Power

One of the essential concepts in understanding the differences in the way men and women communicate is the concept of *team*.

If you ask a group of men their definition of a Team Player, you will likely hear something like this:

A Team Player is someone who knows their role on the team and plays it well.

If you ask the same question to a group of women, their answer would be something like this:

A Team Player is willing to do whatever is needed to support the team.

On the surface, those answers seem similar, but they are very different definitions. The response from the men implies several things. 1. There is a hierarchy. 2. A good team player understands where they fit in the hierarchy in relation to the others on the team. 3. A good team player performs their role well.

Contrasting the women's example to the men's, we can see that it shows a more supportive stance where the focus is on the team as a whole rather than the individual's role. In the female example, there is no evidence of a hierarchy. A good team player is willing to fill whatever role needed to benefit the team—not necessarily a role they do best. A good team player may wear several hats.

In her book *Hardball for Women: Winning at the Game of Business*, Dr. Pat Heim introduces the "power dead even" Rule. She writes:

"Girls grow up in flat organizations rather than hierarchies. They learn to cooperate within this structure. Rather than having a coach or top banana tell them what to do, girls cooperate in a web of relationships for the sake of preserving the friendship. It doesn't take long for a little girl to discover that if she wants to be the leader and she starts pushing her playmates around, relationships will suffer; friends will call her bossy and avoid her. As a result, she tries to keep the power dead even."

Women will purposely do activities or say things that lower themselves in the hierarchy to make others (male or female) feel more comfortable or preserve a relationship. They are often unaware of how their behaviors may be perceived or why it would be a concern.

Here is an example from my experience that may help you recognize how this behavior could manifest in a modern workplace.

I was with a group of my work colleagues at a business event. The event took place at a facility with meeting rooms and an arcade. At a break, we were given quarters and told to go play to burn off some steam before our next meeting. I entered the arcade and found several of my male peers already playing a video game called "Downhill Racer." It involved leaning from side to side and racing for the best time to complete a virtual downhill ski run.

As Jack's avatar swished from side to side down the virtual hill, he leaned around the console and yelled, "Hey Jill, come over here and play with us! I bet I can kick your ass at this game!"

"Ok, I haven't played that one before, but I will give it a try."

Jack crashed through several gates and finally finished his downhill run, laughing and cheering. "Your Turn—let's see what you've got!"

I took over the console and began my downhill racing descent. As I suspected, I wasn't a natural at online downhill racing. Of course, Jack hadn't been brilliant either. He continued poking fun at me as I crashed through gates, veered at crazy angles, and laughed at my sad attempt. All the laughing made my poor racing avatar swerve at even worse angles! Jack and I continued playing for a while and were laughing loudly when our coworker, Louise, walked up.

I motioned for her, "Hey, Louise! Come play with us—it's fun!"

"Oh, no," she shook her head. "I am not any good at that game."

"You can't be any worse than me," I was still laughing from my terrible run down the hill. "Just watch how bad I am at this!"

Let's break down this scene. First, Jack challenged me to come and compete with him. His goal was to invite a friend to play a game, to have fun, and to keep having a fun time himself. Later, I invited Louise to come and play, implying that I wanted her to join in on the fun but *not* asking her to compete with me. Additionally, Louise told me that she was not good at the game (which is similar to my initial response to Jack), and I identified with her by attesting to my own lack of skill.

Instead of challenging her lack of confidence, which Jack did with me, I let Louise know that I would not compete with her and restated that I was bad at the game, too—the implication was that she would be in like company by playing with me. It's interesting to note that even if I *were* good at the game, I would have downplayed it, so Louise would want to join in on the fun.

I was not aware of it at the time, but I lowered myself in the informal hierarchy to make her feel comfortable enough to join us. I valued her friendship and wanted to preserve it. It would be a mistake to interpret our behavior as a lack of confidence or competitiveness. Jack invited me as a friend through a friendly ribbing. I invited Louise as a friend through similitude. Both are normal ways for the respective genders to communicate.

Brain Science

Brain imaging technology has come a long way in the last ten years and has allowed us to better understand the differences in how the brains of men and women process information. Studies (Zaidi, 2010, Ingalhalikar et al., 2013) have found striking differences in the neural wiring of men and women.

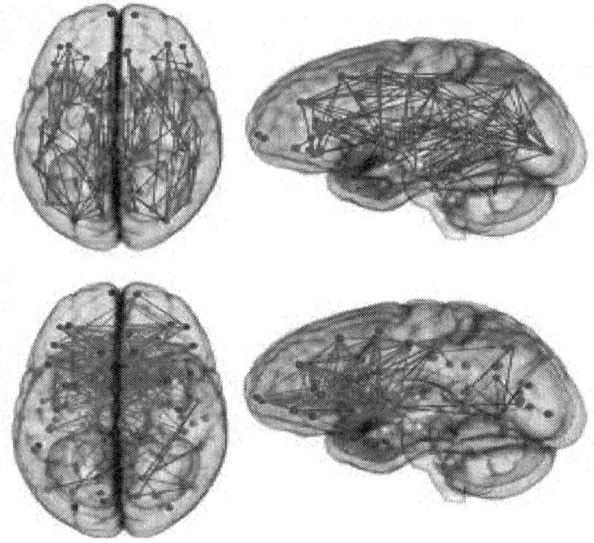

CREDIT: RAGINI VERMA, PHD, PROCEEDINGS OF THE
NATIONAL ACADEMY OF SCIENCES

The studies showed that men had greater connectivity within each hemisphere, and women had better connectivity across hemispheres, as seen in the diagram (male brain on the top portion, female brain on the lower portion). As a result of these differences, researchers concluded that men are better at performing a single task, and women are better at multitasking and memory.

"It's quite striking how complementary the brains of women and men really are," study co-author Dr. Ruben Gur, a Psychology professor and the Director of the Brain Behavior Laboratory at the University of Pennsylvania, said in a press release.

One of the more fun analogies made to understand these brain differences is in the book *Men Are Like Waffles, Women Are Like Spaghetti* by Bill and Pam Farrel. They propose that a man's brain operates much like a waffle, with rows of boxes running both horizontally and vertically. They argue that men put their lives, issues, and responsibilities in distinct boxes in the waffle. They will enter a box, solve any issues there, then move on to the next box in a logical order.

Men also have what is described as a "Nothing" box. While the box is not always completely empty (it might contain something trivial), these boxes are where a man's brain can rest without problem-solving. Women can sometimes tell when a man has gone to a resting place in his mind and will often ask what they are thinking. The Farrels describe such an interaction where the wife asks her husband what he is thinking. The husband panics because if he tells her exactly what he was thinking about (the world series, pitching stats, dinosaurs, time travel…something trivial), she may think he is lying. If he says nothing, she might think he is hiding something. Either way, she will be suspicious because she cannot imagine a moment when her mind is at rest. Literally thinking of nothing is a foreign concept to most women.

Women's brains are simply not wired that way. They are always looking for connections, so the concept is unfathomable to most women. One of the most stressful things you can say to a woman is, "Relax, just empty your mind." That usually sparks an eruption of thoughts (and stomach acid).

To further the analogy, the Farrels go on to describe how women are like spaghetti. If you look at a plate of spaghetti, you notice that every noodle intertwines with every other noodle. They explain that women attempt to connect every thought with every other thought. When women work through a problem, they will often talk things through with others, as it helps them connect the logical, emotional, relational, and spiritual aspects of the problem.

I find it helpful to visualize the brain as a complex spreadsheet with multiple tabs. Each tab of the spreadsheet contains thousands of rows and columns of data. Men tend to process the data deeply within each tab before moving to the next tab on the spreadsheet. This makes men more effective at learning and performing a single complex task. Women, on the other hand, tend to process data points across the tabs of the spreadsheet, often in a non-linear fashion. This allows women to have better memory and social cognition skills, making them more equipped for multitasking and creating intuitive solutions that work for a group.

Chapter Summary

- Boys' traditional childhood games help them gain more experience navigating a structural hierarchy, competing, and aggressiveness. Girls' childhood play gives them more experience interacting with others, talking, sharing feelings, and taking turns.

- Boys will often have friends on the opposing team, and they will be on the same team with people that they don't like. They learn to resolve disputes on the playing field and resume their friendships once the game is over. Girls typically only play with other children they like. Those friendships continue even when the play activity is completed.

- Men need to understand where they are in the hierarchy, and they will avoid activities that they perceive could lower them in the hierarchy.

- Women will purposely do or say things that will lower themselves in the hierarchy to make others feel more comfortable or to maintain relationships. This keeps the power dead even.

- Brain imaging studies show that men have greater connectivity within each hemisphere of the brain, while women had better connectivity across hemispheres. As a result, men are better at performing a single task, and women are better at multitasking and memory.

Impact at Work

2

PERFORMANCE AND PROMOTION

The *Women in the Workplace 2019* study (McKinsey & Company and Leanin.org) included 329 companies and surveyed more than 68,500 men and women about their workplace experiences. Researchers received very different answers from men, women, and HR leaders when collecting data about the biggest challenge facing businesses in achieving equal numbers of women and men in management positions.

HR Leaders said that the biggest challenge was that women don't get enough sponsorship. Men said the biggest challenge was that there are too few qualified women in the pipeline. Women said the biggest challenge was that women are judged by different standards. All participants saw the issue through different lenses or "gender goggles."

This section of the book will explore the gender communication style differences that can impact the workplace. Just like differences in personality, there are no right or wrong behaviors, but it helps to recognize the different styles of others.

Promoting Accomplishments

Men tend to self-promote their accomplishments while working with their leaders, while women tend to promote their performance less and expect their performance to speak for itself. The differences in play and games found in the genders during childhood echoes into adulthood, showing up in both formal and informal ways.

In the *Harvard Business Review* study, "Why Don't Women Self-Promote as Much as Men?" they found a significant gender gap in self-promotion. They concluded that women provided less favorable assessments of their own past performance than equally performing men. The studies were conducted with two levels of transparency, one that the participants knew was public (others saw the ratings) and one that was private (only researchers saw the ratings). In both studies, the gender gap persisted even though men and women performed equally well. The gender difference was most pronounced in the public study. Men in the public version rated themselves an average of 61 out of 100, while women only rated themselves a 46 out of 100. This is consistent with the foundational hierarchy concept that men try to maintain their status in public as high as possible on the informal hierarchy.

I distinctly remember a time where this difference played out in front of me. I'd walked into a common gathering area at the front of a co-location space. Three men were standing in the hallway, talking as I came closer to the group.

Jack looked at George and asked, "Have you ever played at the XYZ Country Club?"

George stood a little taller and exclaimed, "Yes, I had my best game ever there! I pitched it into the hole straight from the end of the green on the seventh hole. It was amazing!"

Jack's voice rose louder as he replied, "Well, you should have seen the fifty-foot putt I made on the tenth hole. It was epic!"

The third man, Benjamin, jumped into the conversation excitedly and almost shouted, "I was there the year that Tiger won the PGA Championship, and I got special VIP passes to the meet and greet party. Tiger gave me a few pointers on how to make those championship shots!"

They were each trying to "one-up" each other with their golf experience, as is typical for men in the workplace. They saw me walk past them, smiling at their banter, and quickly changed the subject to something work-related.

Benjamin then looked at Jack and said, "Hey, was the project launched yesterday?"

"Yes," Jack replied. "I'm surprised you didn't hear about it. It went better than expected. All the users got their work done ten times faster than normal."

"That's great!" Benjamin grinned. "Was it as smooth as the rollout that we worked on together last year?"

"Even smoother!"

Again—bragging was used as a form of camaraderie building. Jack was thrilled to share his successful presentation, and Benjamin was happy to celebrate the win with him while mentioning his own win in the past. It's right on the money for typical male conversation.

Later that same day, I overheard two women talking in the same location as the men had been earlier. Mary, a female team leader, was talking about her team's project with Thelma.

"How did your launch go yesterday?" Thelma asked Mary, upbeat and seemingly hopeful for good news.

Mary sighed deeply. "Oh, it went pretty well. The system is up and running now, but my team was up most of the night fixing last-minute issues so that the users would not feel the impact this morning. We are all exhausted!"

Thelma nodded, "I'm sorry to hear that you guys had a rough night." The sympathy was evident in her tone. "But it sounds like it went smooth from the user standpoint, and that's a good thing! I know how frustrating nights like that are, something similar happened to my team a couple of months ago."

The conversation evolved, and Thelma later shared a similar experience with Mary, identifying with her struggles.

Interestingly, both Mary and Jack were describing the same project launch. Each person gave an accurate description, but Jack's focus was on the final *accomplishment*, and Mary's focus was on the *process* the team went through to make it successful.

Style difference can also be seen in the way employees provide updates to their leaders. Men often casually drop in to see their leaders (both male and female) early in the morning or later in the evening to chat; they tend to build rapport and mention their accomplishments. They also try to compliment the leader with phrases like "great presentation," or "I really like the new strategy."

When they talk to their leader about their accomplishments, men will often use the word "I," even when a larger team is involved. This is not a conscious attempt to steal credit or undermine others; it is merely a linguistic habit harboring no ill intent.

Additionally, women prefer more formal ways of communicating status to avoid the appearance of bragging. They are also cautious about approaching male leaders casually outside of normal work hours or complimenting them to avoid any appearance of impropriety. Women tend to speak using the word "we," even when referring to an individual accomplishment.

The differences in the use of the "I" and "we" pronouns can also be observed when interviewing candidates. Male candidates often describe their accomplishments using "I," and female candidates often use "we." Trained interviewers know that it is important to ask follow-up questions to determine the candidate's actual role in the accomplishment.

These style differences can lead to situations where leaders and interviewers know more about the males' accomplishments. It can also lead to confusion or conflict about who should get the credit for an accomplishment.

Regardless of gender, is it important for all employees to find a way to regularly update leadership on their accomplishments and give appropriate credit for work completed with the help of others. Here are some tips to keep your leader informed:

- Set up a regular weekly (in person or video chat) update with your leader to inform them of status. Focus on the accomplishments, not the issues that cropped up along the way. If you are working with others, be sure to mention the contributions of coworkers. Avoid surprises by keeping them informed.

- Email late-breaking news notices whenever some good news or long-awaited progress happens on a project.

- If you receive a thank-you note from a coworker or customer, forward it to your boss with a header that says something like, "Just received this nice note from a customer, thought you would enjoy seeing some good news today!"

- If you are in the same location as your leader, find a good time to connect and get to know each other better informally. This is typically before work, during lunch hour or after work. Talk about rapport building topics (families, good books to read, movies, hobbies, but avoid talking about frustrations or issues). You can casually mention progress on a project, but that isn't the focus of the conversation.

Feedback

Everyone needs to receive detailed feedback in order to show improvement. The Center for Talent Innovation reports that women are 32% less likely than men to receive *any* feedback from male leaders. In addition, the *Harvard Business Review* article, "Research: Vague Feedback Is Holding Women Back" describes an analysis of performance reviews of men and women in similar roles across three high-tech companies. The data showed that the feedback women *do* receive is less likely to be tied to business outcomes and more likely to be about their communication style.

The article further stated that women were two times more likely than men to receive feedback about being too aggressive. With phrases like "your speaking style is off-putting." Women's positive feedback was also two times more likely to contain words like collaborative, helpful, and supportive. Conversely, men's positive feedback contained twice as many words related to assertiveness, independence, and self-confidence. Men also received three times more feedback than women linked to specific business outcomes.

A study on gender stereotypes in the workplace (Heilman, 2012) evaluated both descriptive gender stereotypes (designating what women and men *are* like) and prescriptive gender stereotypes (designating what women and men *should be* like). They found evidence that while these biases are improving over time, they still exist in the workplace. The biases show up in the feedback, as described above. For example, the woman's feedback about being too aggressive or off-putting can be a result of prescriptive bias. The woman is not behaving in the way the leader expects a woman to behave, and she is thus penalized. The same type of bias and punishment can be seen for men that exhibit behaviors that lower them in the hierarchy.

In my first performance evaluation of my career, I received feedback that I was not assertive enough. My second performance evaluation said I was too assertive. Oops...I may have overcorrected and changed my behavior too dramatically. It's also possible that as a female, I behaved more assertively than was expected of me at that time. I was too immature in my career to know that I should ask my leader for examples of the specific behaviors to be modified. I didn't understand the "appropriate" level of assertiveness until much later in my career. This illustrates the struggle that many women try to balance. An assertive woman may be viewed as abrasive and bossy, but a friendly, collaborative woman may be considered too soft and not taken seriously.

Most of my performance appraisals for the first twelve years of my career were variations on the theme of assertiveness and speaking up in meetings. It was at that point in my career when Bob became my leader. Bob is a master at giving and receiving feedback, as evidenced by the dozens of people who became masters of their work under his leadership.

For one, Bob was a terrific people leader because he made developing the people on his team a priority. He measured his success as a leader by how many people on his team he could promote to bigger jobs. Interestingly, Bob's development process was consistent for all employees on his team, both male and female.

Additionally, Bob gave detailed and timely feedback and not just during the annual performance appraisals. He pointed out real, tactical ways to be more effective and have more executive presence. Bob provided constructive feedback as soon as possible after a coachable situation occurred, and his developmental feedback was *always* given in private while praise was usually given in public. The best part about his feedback was that it was actionable. He would say something like, "In this specific situation, I expected to see this, but I saw that instead. The next time this situation occurs, I would like to see you do this."

Finally, Bob pioneered a unique annual process to enable his employees to learn and grow from their annual reviews. He surpassed what HR required and asked his employees to fill out a self-assessment on the behaviors he expected to see from the team's leaders.

Once year, I filled out my self-assessment while he filled out his assessment of me on those same behaviors. We sent them to each other before the evaluation meeting so that I could read it over and process it before we talked with each other formally. During the evaluation, we discussed the areas where our perceptions were different. This particular year, Bob rated me lower than I expected in an area. He said he did not see me displaying the behavior. I told him that I was doing that behavior, and his response was, "then you must not be communicating to me about it." He was right! I was expecting him to know about my actions without telling him explicitly about them.

HR required all employees to list out their accomplishments each year. Bob would review my accomplishments and give them the "so what?" test. He would not let me submit the evaluation until my accomplishments were tied to the specific business outcomes and clearly articulated the impact I made. Without his direct feedback and coaching, I am doubtful I would have made it to the executive level in my career.

Bob's people development style is a great example for leaders to follow on how to give feedback to their employees that will help them improve their performance and get promoted regardless of gender. Employees who aren't lucky enough to have a leader like Bob should request ongoing, accurate, and timely feedback to clarify what needs to change to achieve their career goals. They should also provide their leader with a summary of how their accomplishments made a difference to the company's metrics, even if their manager is not asking for one.

Sharing Emotions

It is common for women to reveal hopes, concerns, and feelings to express solidarity with others. As a result, women tend to be more open with the full range of emotions in the workplace, including excitement, tiredness, frustration, anger, annoyance, and disappointment.

The book *Hardball for Women: Winning at the Game of Business*, explains how women share information and feelings to establish closeness with others, even people they don't know well.

In contrast, men express a narrower range of emotions in the workplace, primarily anger and frustration. Even though the men's emotional range was more restricted, the UK Job Board Totaljobs study found that men showed more emotion than women at work, mostly expressed as anger. Specifically, men got angry when they were criticized, when their ideas were not heard, or when they got in an argument.

In my own experience, both as an employee and as a leader, I found that women openly share frustrations and challenges to build rapport with their leader. This can backfire whether their leader is male or female.

One day, I sat in my office working on my computer, when one of my employees, Nisha, knocked on my door. I turned to face her and motioned for her to sit down across from me. Her face and her eyes were red as if she had cried recently.

Nisha sat down with a sigh, "Do you have a few minutes? I just need to talk."

"Sure, what's on your mind?" I mentally braced for the bad news that might be coming.

"My daughter is driving me crazy—she won't listen to me! My husband is out of town, and my dog is sick, and I feel so overwhelmed."

I listened as Nisha went on to describe her difficult family situation in detail, nodding my head and occasionally stopping her to ask clarifying questions.

Realizing time was likely slipping away from Nisha as she vented the goings-on in her personal life, I asked her the time of her next meeting because I knew I had another meeting coming up and suspected she did as well.

"Oh! I have to go! Thanks for listening," she said as she picked up her cell phone and ran to her next meeting.

It was not the first time that Nisha had sought me out as a listening ear. A few weeks later, a great special project came up that was perfect for Nisha's skillset. Because of our conversations, I admit that I hesitated a little before assigning the project to her. It crossed my mind that since she felt so overwhelmed, it might be poor timing for her to take on a new project. I immediately recognized that it was not my responsibility to determine that for her. I offered her the project and let her decide what she could handle.

If Nisha had shared the same personal information with a male leader, there could be an additional reaction. Since it is uncommon for men to share emotions to build connection, his first reaction may be to offer solutions (take work off her plate, give advice, etc.). She may get frustrated because she wasn't seeking a solution. Even though male leaders are more likely to jump in to fix an issue, women leaders can also shift into fix-it mode. It is the nature of a leadership role to remove barriers for employees to complete their work. It is natural for all leaders to default to help mode vs. listen mode.

As a result, when someone shares concerns with a leader, it is a good practice for leaders to ask, "Are you looking for help, or do you just want me to listen?"

For employees, it is important to find someone they can trust to share concerns and frustrations. However, it is best if that person is a friend or peer rather than their leader.

While we are on the topic of emotions, let me touch on the topic of tears. After presenting this gender information to a group of male leaders, I am often asked, "What am I supposed to do when a female employee starts crying?" My response is always, "What do you do when a male employee starts crying?" Many times, they answer, "I have never had that situation." This usually means they haven't been a leader very long because I have had men cry in my office many times over the years, although not nearly as frequently as women.

In the *Forbes* article, "The Surprising Truth about Crying at Work," Melody Wilding states:

"Women are biologically hardwired to cry more frequently than men. They have six times the amount of prolactin, which is a hormone related to crying, than men, so it's no surprise that women sometimes feel tears come to their eyes during inopportune moments. In fact, research shows that 41% of women have cried at work at some point during their careers. This statistic is a reminder of something we often forget: crying is an evolutionary process, and we don't have a whole lot of control over when it happens (if any—have you ever tried to stop yourself from crying once the floodgates have opened?). Crying has nothing to do with mental toughness and everything to do with biology."

So, what should happen when someone starts crying? It is best to simply treat them with the same respect and dignity you would want in that situation. Offer them a tissue and ask them if they would like a few minutes to gather themselves. After they are ready to proceed, continue like nothing happened, and don't bring it up again. Crying in front of your boss is awkward and embarrassing—the less fuss made about it, the better.

What if you are the one who starts crying in front of your boss? That happened to me when I was working for Bob. I'd received a call from home about a family member that upset me. As I hung up and started for the door, tears were already coming down my face when my leader, Bob, cheerily walks into my office and inadvertently blocked my doorway. He'd started asking me questions about a project, then he looked up and noticed my face. Of course, this just made the tears come harder, and I couldn't speak. I shook my head, waved my arm, and bolted past him as I ran to the ladies' room. I spent about 10–15 minutes in the ladies' room regaining my composure.

Afterward, I went to Bob's office and said, "You had some questions for me about the project?" He looked at me, smiled, and proceeded to ask his questions like nothing had happened. I was thankful that he ignored the whole situation.

The best way to handle being overcome with tears is to find a way to regain composure. Every person and situation is different, but give yourself permission to do what is needed to regroup.

Asking Questions

Who asks more questions, men or women? In the June 2019 issue of *Behavioral Scientist*, Elizabeth Weingarten presents her findings on that question. She concludes that in high-stakes settings (industry conferences, high-level meetings, etc.), men tend to ask more questions, while in a smaller group or interpersonal settings, women tend to ask more questions.

Asking questions in a high-stakes meeting is consistent with men's desire to be seen and impart knowledge to improve their hierarchy status. However, men tend to ask fewer questions of their leader, because they are aware that the behavior can be perceived as putting them lower in the informal hierarchy. As a result, they also tend to wait longer to escalate issues to their leadership. A study published in the October 2015 *The Leadership Quarterly* confirmed that asking questions and seeking help lowers the employee's competence rating (as rated by his leader), even though those behaviors are recognized as necessary for effective performance.

For women, asking questions in small group settings is consistent with their desire to collaborate and explore data options with others. Women ask more questions in one-on-one meetings with their leaders, as they are not as concerned about their status in the hierarchy. They may also bring options to their leader hoping to collaborate, weigh the options, and come up with the best solution together.

The potential impact of this gender difference was brought to my attention while on an interview team for a technical position. I had prior experience with both candidates who were finalists for the job (one male, one female), as they had both worked for me in the past. The interview team was debriefing after the interviews, discussing the candidate we thought would be the best fit for the role.

A male member of the interview team confidently stated that Johan was the best candidate.

I asked him why.

He looked at me across the table, seemingly a bit annoyed at my question. "Mary isn't as technically strong as Johan."

I raised my eyebrows and looked at him quizzically and asked, "They have similar backgrounds. What makes you say that?"

He seemed to grow larger in his chair as he leaned forward, raised his voice slightly, and said, "I have worked with both Mary and Johan, and Mary asked a lot more questions and needed more validation than Johan."

I, too, leaned forward, raised my voice slightly, and replied, "I have also worked with both Mary and Johan, and Mary's technical skills are just as strong as Johan's." I also remembered that Mary had an open, collaborative style that included asking questions and weighing options out loud as she worked on the best solution with her peers.

Fortunately, the hiring manager noticed the escalation of voices and asked us to move on to evaluate other qualification areas. At the end of the discussion, Mary was selected for the job because she had some other qualifications that Johan did not have. However, had everything else been equal, there is a chance that she might not have gotten the job. Her style of asking questions and collaborating on data options had been misinterpreted as having weaker technical skills and a need for validation.

When asking our leaders questions, it is important to only ask questions that need to be answered at that leader's level. This will demonstrate resourcefulness and an appreciation for the value of the leader's time. Consider this conversation that I had with my leader, Bob.

Bob sent me an email stating, "There is a conference coming up in January, and we have to present our best practices on our new ABC process. You are the expert in this area, so you should plan to go and present."

I was excited to hear about this conference, but I had a few questions. So, I sent this email reply, "What is the date and location of the conference? Do I need approval of the content before the conference?"

I waited a couple of days and received no emails back from Bob. I assumed it must have gotten lost in his inbox. The next time I saw him in the hallway, I said, "Hey, Bob, did you see the questions I emailed to you about the conference?"

Bob stared at me briefly before saying, "You should talk to the admin about those." Then he turned and walked away. I stood there, stunned, and tried to figure out what had just happened. It took me a few minutes to understand that Bob told me in a not-so-subtle way that those details were not relevant to him, and I should seek the answer to those types of questions from his admin.

I have experienced "non-response" emails from Bob a few other times over my career, and they almost always meant that I should not have asked him that question. This was Bob's method of coaching me on the types of questions that should go to him and those that should not. Very few leaders provide this type of coaching, and I appreciated him taking the time to make me aware.

While playing games as children, many men were socialized not to question the leader in public. Although coaching styles are evolving to be less directive over time, this dynamic may still be seen in the workplace. When a leader (male or female) is questioned, especially in front of others, there may be a perception that the person asking the question is challenging the leader's authority, not merely looking for clarification on a task. While asking questions is an important process, every leader has a different tolerance level for them. It is better to ask a trusted coworker most questions and save only the critical ones for a leader. If a leader assigns a task that requires clarification, it is better to get clarification in a private one-on-one meeting, so as not to appear to be challenging their authority in public.

Decision Making and Giving Directions

When it comes to making decisions, men tend to ask for less input than women before deciding. In 2015, Chris Gerneich and Christina Exner conducted a study that found women gather information for decision-making from more varied sources than men. This finding is consistent with the brain science discussed in previous chapters. Women seek to connect multiple data points from various sources, similar to connecting data across multiple tabs of a spreadsheet.

The style that works best for decision making depends primarily on the type of decision that needs to be made. If the decision requires a lot of buy-in to implement, it is a good idea to collect more input. If the decision requires no buy-in (i.e., deciding who is assigned a parking space), less input is better.

If a male employee has never worked with a female leader before, her requests for more pre-decision input could confuse him, and he might perceive her as indecisive. If he concludes she is indecisive, he may start pushing on other boundaries to determine his level in the hierarchy.

The situation can be further complicated if the female leader is not direct in her instructions to him on what she wants him to complete. Women tend to give directions using a more indirect communication style, using fillers and hedges to soften the communication. In "Interpersonal Communication: Competence and Contexts," Shelly Lane found that women use more indirect language when asking others to do things. For example, a woman may say, "it sure is hot in here," which could be an implied request to turn on the air conditioning.

If a request is made using indirect language in the workplace, there is a chance it may be misinterpreted.

Men tend to be very direct when asking for a task to be completed, and in extreme cases, they can be perceived as a bully. Women tend to use more filler words in their requests, and in extreme cases, that can lead to unclear or overly softened requests. Both men and women should give directions clearly with specific deadlines and using the appropriate tone to avoid this issue. It is also helpful to send out meeting notes that highlight action items with owners and expected completion dates.

Chapter Summary

- When working with leaders, men tend to self-promote their accomplishments, while women tend to promote their performance less and expect their performance to speak for itself.

- Men receive more feedback related to business outcomes than women. Women are more likely to receive feedback on their communication styles.

- Women tend to be more open in the workplace with their full range of emotions, while men typically only express anger or frustration. Women share feelings and concerns to connect with others.

- Men tend to ask more questions in large, high stakes settings; women tend to ask more questions in small group settings.

- Women tend to collect more inputs before decision making than men.

- Men tend to be more direct in giving instructions; women use more indirect language and fillers.

3

WORKING TOGETHER

Trust

Just as men and women have different definitions for a team player, they also have different definitions of trust. In the book, *Hardball for Women: Winning at the Game of Business*, this difference is described as:

"Men trust someone whom they perceive will not ridicule them or divulge what they say to others. Women see trust as carrying out your word or promise."

A woman can do everything she committed to do, and a man still may not trust her if he is concerned that she will talk badly about him to others. Sometimes you will hear this referred to in terms of respect. Men tend to trust people who do what they say *and* do not talk badly about them to others. Women tend to trust people based primarily on their ability to keep their promises and commitments.

While all humans want to be respected and admired, men have a more profound need for admiration, especially in public. That is why it is very damaging to their trust if they perceive that others are talking badly about them and, of course, it lowers them in the informal hierarchy. Women are often surprised that men have this strong need for admiration in public. A well placed, sincere compliment to a male can have a powerful effect on building a relationship with him. As mentioned in the section on Promoting Accomplishments, men understand this and will often compliment their leaders.

My leader, Bob, reported directly to the CEO, and he asked me to attend a meeting with him to give an update about a large project that my team was responsible for delivering. As Bob introduced me, he accidentally told the CEO that the project would be completed in June instead of the real date of September. I was in a dilemma over whether or not I should have interrupted and told the CEO that Bob was mistaken versus staying quiet and taking the consequences later when he assumed the project was three months late. I chose to remain quiet, and immediately after the meeting, I went to Bob and stated cautiously, "The date you gave on the project completion was actually three months too early. It will be done in September, not June."

Bob looked at me curiously before saying, "Ok, thanks for telling me," and started walking down the hallway.

I increased my pace until I walked beside him and then stopped and looked Bob in the eyes and asked, "I'm interested in your feedback, did I handle that situation appropriately? Should I have interrupted and corrected the date in the meeting?"

"No," he smiled at me. "And thank you for not making me look bad in front of my boss! That is a golden rule. You should never make anyone look bad in front of their boss."

Still concerned about the date mix-up, I asked, "What do I need to do to fix the situation?"

Bob grew serious, "Nothing. If he remembers the date, I will tell him that I might have given him the wrong date, but most likely, he won't remember it. Either way, I have your back. I won't tell him that the team was late. I will own my mistake if necessary."

I smiled, let out the breath I didn't realize I was holding, and said, "Thank you for saying that. It makes me feel a lot better!"

I know the situation above helped me build trust with Bob. He knew I would not speak badly in front of his boss, and true to his word, the team was never accused of lateness on the project.

Conflict

In the workplace, men and women may face conflicts because of their communication style differences. They may also react differently to conflict and solve it using different methods.

A woman's ability to connect disparate data sources is one example of a style difference that may cause conflict. This is recognized as a highly valued skill to bring to a team. However, if the wrong conclusions are drawn from the data or someone's intentions are misunderstood, that often leads to conflict.

I worked for a company that was in the middle of a difficult year and needed to identify ways to cut costs from the budget. At a budget meeting, there was a lot of debate and hashing out ideas to cut costs when two of my colleagues, Thelma and Carl, had a brief tiff.

Thelma offered an idea, "We should consider delaying the XYZ project and freeing up the consultants."

Carl tensed his shoulders, leaned back in his chair, and said, "I don't see how you can say that. If you decide to go down that path, you are on your own."

One sentence from Carl was all it took for Thelma to become visibly angry. After the meeting ended, she came to my office to discuss the meeting and the comment that Carl made that set her fuming. She had interpreted his statement to mean that, if she pursues her idea, then she would be on her own with no support from him or anyone else on the team. I didn't agree with her interpretation because Carl's statement seemed vague to me.

What I didn't know at the time were the data points Thelma was connecting that enabled her to jump to the conclusion she did. In essence, they'd butted heads earlier about budget cut ideas, so she assumed that Carl nixing her ideas was an overarching theme in their interpersonal relationship. I encouraged Thelma to talk to him directly about it.

They discussed privately, and Carl clarified that, because they had some shared contractors who would not be able to be let go, he would not be able to contribute to the cost cut she suggested. That was why he said she was on her own. It wasn't personal at all, and Thelma had connected the dots to misinterpret a personal slight.

It is common in the workplace for a female employee to collect multiple data points from interactions with a male employee, and then connect those dots to conclude that he is trying to manipulate or undermine her work. In these situations, the best approach is always to clarify with the coworker directly and avoid discussing the concerns with other coworkers.

The way men and women react to conflict may also be different. Men can fight all day and leave immediately to get a beer together. Women, on the other hand, may take conflict very seriously and personally.

A study published in the *Harvard Gazette*, "Resolving Conflict: Men vs. Women" August 2016, looked at men and women's sports and found clear differences in how quickly each gender reconciled with their opponents after a competition.

As children, boys often played against their friends on opposing teams, but once the game was over, they resumed their friendship. For girls, there are no boundaries to friendships. They are loyal friends on and off the field, and they typically don't choose to play with people they don't like. Of course, there is no option to only "play" with those we like in the adult world. Men are friendly at work, but their true friendships are usually outside of work. Women build real friendships both inside and outside of the workplace.

I was in a team meeting with Bob and all of his direct reports. It was one of those all-day strategy planning sessions with a dinner to follow. The meeting had been contentious all day, and by the afternoon, everyone was exhausted and angry. The time came for us to leave for the team dinner. The men patted each other on the back as they left the meeting room and said, "See you at the bar."

Meanwhile, I was not at all in the mood to leave immediately to have dinner with the same people I had just spent hours fighting. I decided to go back to my desk and see if I could process some of what I had heard and ease my blood pressure back down to normal. After about 30 minutes, I decided I had better leave, or be late for dinner. When I arrived at the restaurant, I saw that the other female leader in the meeting had arrived at the same time.

I waved her over, "Hey, I see you are late arriving too. Now we can go in together."

"Yes, I was so mad, I had to go back to my office to process before I could stand to come and eat dinner with everyone!" she replied, walking over to join me.

Both Louise and I had experienced the same meeting and, without knowing it, had both retreated to our offices to cool down before the dinner. It may take time for a woman to process a conflict and move on to be able to interact with those involved, and even longer for her to reset back to friendship.

This processing time is crucial for women. If someone tries to interrupt during the processing, they are more likely to get yelled at or receive the silent treatment. If you come across a female who is in the middle of processing, it is best to either give her space or say, "I see you are processing something, would you like to talk about it?" This acknowledgment can go a long way toward preventing any unnecessary conflict.

For women, it is essential to try not to take disagreement and conflict personally in the workplace. For men, understanding that women process conflicts differently helps maintain relationships.

One thing we all share— we must learn to work with people who we don't like. Here are a few tips to make it easier:

- Reflect on what the person does that makes you dislike them. Once you understand exactly which behavior is bothering you, manage your reaction to that behavior.

- Don't talk badly about a coworker to others; this is never helpful.

- Find common interests (travel, food, shows they like to binge-watch, etc.) that you can talk about when you interact with them.

- Acknowledge the situation; talk to the coworker directly and ask for feedback and suggestions on ways to work better together.

- When you disagree and cannot come to a resolution, instead of saying that you will "agree to disagree," instead say, "I see it differently." This phrasing change will sometimes prompt them to ask why, and they are more likely to listen.

If none of the above works, accept the situation, continue to act professionally, and do what needs to be done to do your job well. Leaving a workplace because of conflict should only be considered in extreme situations. There are typically a few people that you don't like every place you work.

Negotiation

People who negotiate for a living (both male and female) are taught the best techniques for their industry, product, or service. As a result, gender differences in negotiation styles don't show up as frequently.

One area that differences can be seen is in the willingness to negotiate a time conflict. This was reflected in a conversation that a coworker had with her boss at four in the afternoon on Friday.

"Hi Mary," her team leader said as he walked into her office. "Can you send me the data on the product testing results? I need it by Monday at eight."

Mary stopped what she was doing, turned around to face him, hesitated as if she had something to say. "Um. Yes. I can do that," tension clearly showing in her face.

Her team leader did not know that her mother was sick, and she was jumping on a plane at seven that night and would not return until late on Sunday evening. In order to meet his request, she stayed up most of the night to provide the info to him by his eight in the morning deadline. She found out later that he had not even looked at the data until sometime late Monday afternoon, which made her angry.

Women tend to take a request from a leader as a direct order and do not see it as an opening bid on a negotiation. They will work crazy hours trying to meet deadlines only to find out that the request was an opening bid. If she had viewed it as a negotiation, she could have pushed a little to see if there was any flexibility in the deadline. The conversation would instead look more like this:

"Hi Mary," her team leader said as he walked into her office. "Can you send me the data on the product testing results? I need it by Monday at eight in the morning."

Mary stopped what she was doing, turned around to face him, and replied, "Is eight Monday a hard deadline? I have a situation with my mother that requires me to be in Florida all weekend. I will have it done by then if required, but if you have any flexibility in the deadline, that'd be extremely helpful."

"Ok," he agreed after a brief pause. "If you can send it to me by noon on Monday, that will give me the afternoon to add it to my presentation before Tuesday morning."

"That's a huge help. Thanks! I will have it to you then."

Non-Verbal Cues

Another source of conflict in the workplace can be non-verbal cues. Non-verbal cues are facial expressions and postures that help reveal unspoken thoughts and emotions. A research study (LaFrance & Vial, 2015) found that women pick up on non-verbal cues more easily and interpret them more accurately than men.

Most of us can recall participating in a confusing meeting where it was unclear what happened; we just know that the meeting was not productive.

If you ask the men in the room what happened, they will give you the meeting's content, but when you ask the women, they might give you the "vibe" of the meeting. For example, one of the men might say, "Charlie gave a presentation on the potential XYZ project delay, and it didn't go well." A woman who attended the meeting might say, "The meeting was going fine until Bob questioned Charlie, then Charlie got angry, backed away from the table, and clammed up. After that, everyone else got uncomfortable and started fidgeting."

Both interpretations of the meeting are valuable input and give us a glimpse of the complementary skillsets of each gender.

In a mixed-gender team meeting, I was listening to a coworker, Carl, proposing a strategy he wanted us to adopt. As he spoke, I nodded my head to show that I was paying attention. When he concluded the proposal, I started to ask questions about the proposal and expressed concern with the direction.

Carl's face turned red, his voice got loud, he threw his hands in the air, and he all-but shouted, "How can you disagree now? You were nodding your head the whole time I talked!"

I was surprised at his outburst. Caught off guard, I got a little defensive. A bit more tersely than appropriate, I shot back, "I nodded to show you that I was listening, not because I agree with you. It's called active listening." This was not a proud moment for either Carl or me. I am sure we sounded like siblings squabbling to the rest of the people in the meeting. All that it lacked was us sticking our tongues out at each other.

I was unaware that men do not typically nod their heads to show they are listening; rather, they only nod when they agree. This is an example where awareness of a gender difference has helped me make slight modifications to my non-verbal communication, so I will not be misinterpreted.

Another area of often-misread non-verbal communication is the physical angle of approach. Each gender has a different preference for the angle of approach when walking toward another person. Men tend to stand side-by-side, shoulder-to-shoulder facing the same direction when they talk to each other. Women tend to face each other directly. Talking face-to-face also allows women to gather more non-verbal cues and information.

The April 2014 *Psychology Today* article "Why You Stand Side-By-Side or Face-to-Face," explains that men typically only approach using a direct facing pose when they are in conflict. As a result, if a woman approaches a man to discuss a topic in the direct facing posture, he may instinctively become defensive.

When approaching a man, it is better to approach him from the side or an angle.

Women prefer to be approached from the front and may be uncomfortable when approached from the side or back. This might be because women learn from a young age to be aware of their surroundings and be cautious of anyone approaching them from the side or back for their security.

Chapter Summary

- Men and women have different definitions of trust. Doing what has been committed to builds trust. In addition, for men to fully trust, it is important to them to be shown respect and believe they will not be talked negatively about in public.

- Women can connect disparate data points; however, they sometimes misunderstand someone's intention or language, causing conflict.

- Women tend to take conflict more personally than men do, and it takes a little more time for them to process the conflict and return to friendliness.

- Misreading or misunderstanding non-verbal cues can lead to conflict. It helps to resist the urge to nod the head when listening to a proposal that you disagree with. Also, it is preferable to approach a man from the side or back and a woman from the front.

4

MEETING TOGETHER

Differences in men's and women's interaction styles can be seen when they gather in gendered or mixed-gender groups. In this chapter, we will discuss these style differences and their impact in the workplace.

Group Dynamics

If a group of six men stands in a circle talking animatedly about a topic at a networking event, and a woman walks up and quietly joins the group, what do you think happens next?

I have asked this question to many groups, and almost every woman can tell you that when they join an all-male group, the men will immediately stop talking. The men are usually unaware of this behavior. They will look at the woman joining the group to find out if she has a question or if she plans to join the group.

Now the reverse question:

If a group of six women stands in a circle talking animatedly about a topic, and a man walks up and quietly joins the group. What happens next?

Typically, the women in the group will continue talking, and the group physically opens to make space to accept the new member. They will greet the new member and continue talking unless they perceive the topic might not be appropriate. In that case, they will gradually change the subject. This is done with no perceivable break in the conversation. It doesn't matter if the new person is male or female.

So, the next logical question is:

What happens when someone new approaches a mixed-gender group?

The group tends to behave more like the all-female group and leans toward more inclusive behavior.

I was asked to give a presentation on gender differences to a mixed-gender group of early-career employees. There was a reception before the presentation, and the event organizer wanted to know if we could do an experiment prior to the talk to demonstrate some of the gender differences. We decided to do a variation on the behavior described above to see what would happen.

We divided two groups by gender and gave each group a list of verbs and asked them to decide if they were more masculine or feminine. There were no right answers to this quiz; it was totally made up so that the groups would be busy on a task while we conducted the *real* experiment. Before the meeting, I arranged for one of my male coworkers to join the session late and join the group of women while I planned to join the group of men. We let the groups work until they were deeply engaged in the activity and then joined our respective groups.

When I stepped into the group of men, they were arguing loudly, and they immediately stopped talking and asked me what I wanted. I told them that I was just observing and would like to join their group. They looked at me awkwardly, and one of the more vocal males on the team said, "We are already done" (which I knew not to be true), and the male group dispersed and sat down. I then looked to the other side of the room where the group of women worked with the male coworker who joined late. They were voting on each verb to determine how it should be categorized. My male coworker had not only been readily accepted into the group, but he was also an active voting member!

The results from that brief experiment showed us what we expected about how a same-gender group welcomed a new opposite gender member. What was unplanned was each group quickly adopted a decision-making process. The group of men had, in a very short time, determined an informal hierarchy. One man made many of the decisions and was also the person who addressed me when I joined the group and determined that the group was done with the exercise. The group of women quickly created a voting process that included everyone in the group.

In "Gender and Group Behavior," L.L. Carli presents research on group dynamics, noting that all-female groups tend to be less hierarchical and more collaborative. All-male groups tend to be more hierarchical and demonstrate more aggressive and dominant behaviors. Mixed-gender groups tend to be more collaborative than all-male groups, but less collaborative than all-female groups.

So, how does knowing this information help us? For men, the awareness of this difference may lead to more inclusive group behavior regardless of the group's mix.

For women, awareness of this behavior frees them from worrying about being unwelcome in male groups.

Talking in Meetings

I have heard claims over the years that women talk more (20,000 words) than men (7000 words) based on a book called *The Female Mind* by Louann Brizendine. However, that has not been my experience in the workplace. The rate of talking depends more on the setting and the purpose of the communication. Women do tend to talk more in private and social settings where the focus is on building relationships. Men tend to talk more in public settings where the focus is on displaying knowledge or demonstrating skill.

In fact, a study published in the *American Political Science Review* found that women speak an average of 25% less (and for a shorter duration) than men in mixed-gender meetings. In addition, another study (Hancock & Rubin, 2014) found that men interrupt women speaking 33% more than men speaking in mixed-gender meetings.

While studies have shown that women speak less in meetings, no one claims to have a comprehensive answer as to *why*. One theory suggests that women are more reluctant to speak in meetings because they are concerned about being judged by different rules than men. This theory was developed based on a study (Maxfield, Grenny, & McMillen, 2018) that found women who express a high-stakes emotional disagreement in a meeting are more likely to be judged as angry or losing control. Each participant was rated on competence before and after these incidents. As a result, those women that expressed disagreement received a 35% competency rating drop. When men express a high stakes disagreement, their perceived competency dropped 22%.

This is a classic risk/reward scenario. While it is important to speak up, there is a risk of losing credibility if the wrong tone or words are used.

The study also found that framing statements can help reduce the emotion perception inequity for both genders. A framing statement is a statement made prior to expressing the dissenting option. It can help set the expectations of the listener and demonstrate that the speaker is in control of their emotions. An example of a framing statement is, "I am going to express my opinion very directly. I'll be as specific as possible." If an employee (male or female) uses a framing statement to set expectations before expressing disagreement, that makes others less likely to perceive their behavior as angry or out of control.

For teams to succeed in flat organizations, input and ideas must be heard from everyone. As a result, each meeting attendee should help facilitate making sure that all people have an opportunity to give their input and ideas, regardless of gender, and keep interruptions to a minimum. If there is a leader in the meeting, they have the primary responsibility to facilitate conversation to get optimum results from the meeting.

Mansplaining

In the last decade, the concept of mansplaining has been a much-discussed topic in business forums. According to *Merriam-Webster*, mansplaining is defined as "to explain something to a woman in a condescending way that assumes she has no knowledge about the topic." Rebecca Solnit first introduced this concept in 2008 in her essay *Men Explain Things to Me*, where she tells a story about a man at a party who explained a book to her while she unsuccessfully tried to tell him that she had, in fact, written that book.

Businesswomen have written many articles, and much anecdotal evidence has been shared stating that mansplaining is a problem in modern workplaces. It shows up in the form of men explaining concepts to women in meetings about which they already have expertise.

This is one of those gender differences where awareness of the issue can help men adapt their behavior to avoid the appearance of mansplaining. In the viral BBC article, "Mansplaining, Explained in One Simple Chart," Kim Goodwin provides a simple chart (below) that helps people know if their behavior could be considered mansplaining. The chart seemed to strike a chord with women worldwide. The article acknowledges that anyone, male or female, could display this behavior. Kim effectively summarizes this issue as follows:

"Mansplaining may seem like a trivial issue in isolation, but how we communicate tells other people how much or little they are valued. And in my experience, humans feel better, work more effectively, and behave better when we feel valued ourselves."

Just as men or women can be guilty of mansplaining, both can also be recipients of the behavior. So, what is the best response if someone starts mansplaining? Here are a few suggestions:

- "You are right, that's why I have already..." (then take back control of conversation).

- "I appreciate your help, but I've got this."

- "That comment indicates that it would be helpful to give you more information about my background."

- If it's a chronic issue, talk to the coworker offline, and explain that the comments are not helpful. Discuss different ways to handle future discussions.

Am I mansplaining?

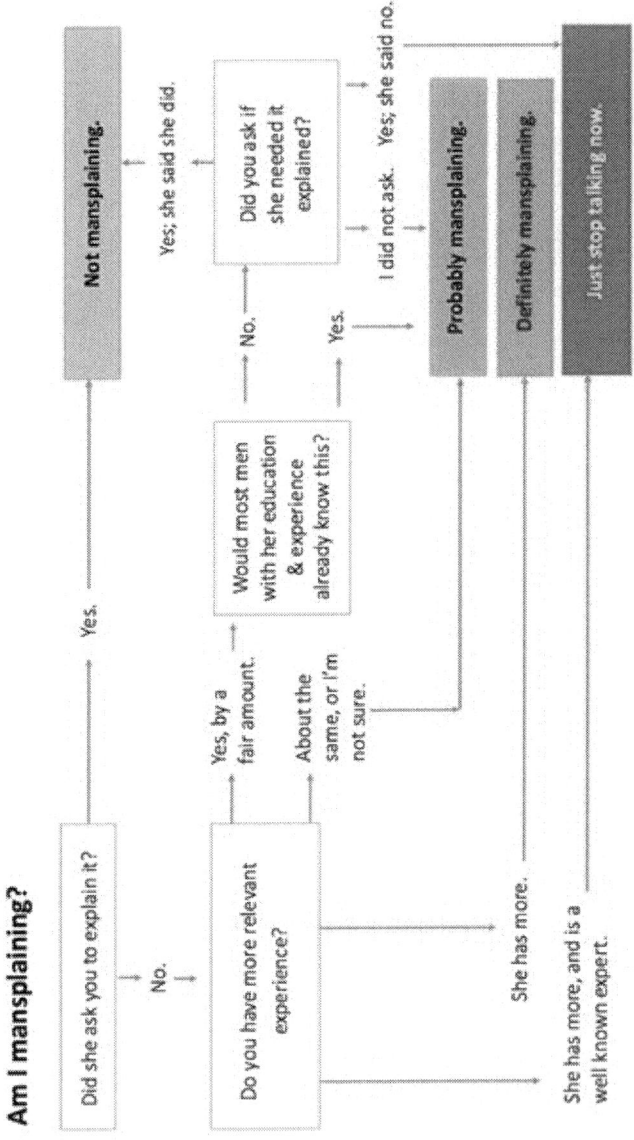

Source: Kim Goodwin.

Influence

Because of their childhood games, men tend to enter the workplace with a better understanding of the unwritten rules of influencing others. Consider this example from early in my career:

I was asked to present a proposal to our CFO about a new process. It was going to require several process changes on his team, and no one was sure how he would react. Since this was a big deal, I decided to ask one of my male peers, Jack, about the best way to approach the presentation. I explained the upcoming presentation to him and asked, "What order should I put the slides in the presentation for the CFO to agree?" The CFO was notorious for making people jump to slides out of order, so I hoped to prevent that.

Jack leaned back in his chair and said, "Before we talk about the specific slides, let's talk about how he and his staff reacted when you had the meeting before the meeting."

"The what?" I was confused.

"The meeting before the meeting. Have you done that yet?"

"I don't know what you are talking about. Can you give me an example?"

"Sure." He leaned forward and put his forearms on his desk as he explained. "Whenever you have a proposal that you know will have some opposition, you meet with each of the key stakeholders first to find out their objections ahead of time. That way, you can address concerns before the meeting.

"Oh, that sounds like a good idea!" I began taking notes, "But will they be surprised if I ask them about the proposal before the meeting?"

Jack chuckled. "They will be surprised if you *don't* ask them about it before the meeting!"

This concept of the meeting before the meeting was a complete revelation. I talked to the CFO's staff and previewed the idea briefly with the CFO so that he would not hear about it for the first time in the meeting. When the time came for the actual meeting, all the pre-work paid off, and the proposal was accepted.

I was grateful to Jack for clueing me into one of the unwritten rules of influence in the workplace. The pre-meeting prevents the leader from hearing about an idea for the first time in public. It also allows for analysis and modification to improve the proposal.

Many women are under the impression that ideas have their own merit and should be discussed and weighed in the meeting with the leader. However, the pre-meeting takes away concerns about hierarchy and allows for better, more honest, analysis of the ideas in a non-public forum.

What surprised me most was when I asked my male peers if they knew about the meeting before the meeting, 100% said, "Yes." When I asked my female peers, all but one of them said, "No."

In the year-long study described in "Success on the Corporate Stage: Why Meetings Matter Even More for Women," they found that most of the men and very few of the women in the study recognized that the meeting before the meeting was "where the real work happens." Another key finding was that important issues are often fully resolved in pre-meeting discussions before the real meeting even starts. As one male executive shared, "The decisions are made in advance, and some women don't seem to know it. This leaves them out of the decision-making."

The pre-meeting is an essential concept that everyone should leverage to their advantage to help influence others.

Honesty and Confidence

When asked a question in a public forum, men may offer their best guess if they are not 100% sure but will say it confidently as if they *did* know for sure. Women, on the other hand, tend to admit that they don't know openly.

Quarterly, the corporate directors had a large meeting to review last quarter's performance. I was attending one of these meetings when the director looked at George, who sat next to me and asked, "What percentage of sales are from category A?"

George leaned forward in his seat and answered confidently, "47%."

After the meeting was over, I leaned over to George and stated, "I'm impressed you knew that number off the top of your head!"

George leaned a little closer and quietly said, "I made it up, but it's probably close."

"What? Seriously?" I exclaimed.

"Yeah, it was my best guess," George answered. "I didn't want to look like I didn't know in front of all these people. He will probably never know the difference, but if he does, at least I will admit the mistake in private."

While I understood the logic that George used, I was shocked that he would do this at such a high-stakes meeting. It turns out that it was precisely because it *was* a high-stakes meeting that he chose to offer his best guess. This behavior is much more common among men than women. Women are more likely to admit that they don't know and offer to respond later.

This example demonstrates the high level of confidence that George had in his ability to assert an answer that was "close," and his willingness to take the calculated risk that he would probably not get caught guessing.

A study (Reuben, Sapienza & Zingales, 2014) found that men showed higher confidence in their performance and rated themselves 30% better than they actually performed on math problems.

Those findings were confirmed in another study (Ehrlinger & Dunning, 2003), which also found that women tend to underestimate their performance in scientific reasoning, even though they performed equally to men. They concluded that women underestimated their performance based on lower levels of confidence.

Demonstrating confidence is a critical skill in the workplace, especially for those wanting to move into leadership roles. It turns out that confidence, even overconfidence, can be beneficial to achieving higher status and promotions.

The Institute for Research on Labor and Employment published a study evaluating the effects of overconfidence. Overconfidence was demonstrated by people who genuinely believed they were more skilled at their jobs than they actually were. They were not faking confidence. The researchers (Anderson, Brion, Moore, & Kennedy, 2012) concluded that overconfident people spoke more often, with confident vocal tone and body language, and provided more information and answers. The participants' overconfidence helped them achieve a higher status.

This is not to suggest that women or men should become overconfident in their abilities to achieve a higher social status. The study was also quick to point out that neither overconfidence nor underestimating ability is the best way to succeed. In the article "Overconfidence" in *Psychology Today*, January 2018, Donald Moore put it this way:

"There is another way—a middle way, between too much and not enough confidence. This Goldilocks zone of confidence is where rational beliefs meet reality. It is fundamentally based on truth and good sense. It is built on beliefs that can be justified by evidence and honest self-examination. It steers between the perilous cliff of overconfidence and the quicksand of under confidence. It is not always easy to find this narrow path; it takes honest self-reflection, level-headed analysis, and the courage to resist wishful thinking."

Exercising honest self-examination can help correct overconfidence, but how can a person build more confidence and correct underconfidence?

According to Katty Kay and Claire Shipman, authors of *The Confidence Code*, the best way to build confidence is to take action, especially when the action involves risk and failure. Doing small things outside our comfort zone can help us start simple and work up to taking bigger risks. For example, if you are uncomfortable around people, try to engage with a stranger the next time you're at a party.

The worst thing that can happen is that we might fail. But if we fail, we will learn from it. We should not ruminate on the failure but move on and try again. It is this repetition that builds our confidence. The great news is that confidence is a learned skill and will improve with practice. The authors do caution that we should not attempt to just "fake it till we make it." There are times we may have to act confident even when we don't feel confident. However, true confidence isn't about pretending; it is gained from genuine accomplishment and work.

It's said that we should do one thing every day that scares us. I haven't quite accomplished that yet. However, one exercise that I have found effective is to sit down once a year and list out three big things that I would like to learn or attempt that year. Things like learn a language, write a book, move to a new job, go on an African safari.

I also make a list of five to ten small things to try that are out of my comfort zone. Things from my lists have been: host a monthly neighborhood party, crochet a baby blanket, learn how to play pickleball, test drive a Tesla using self-drive mode, mentor High School students, and start an herb garden. They each have varying degrees of failure risk. I have a very misshapen baby blanket and a dead herb garden to prove it! And my husband loves to entertain others at parties by telling the story about the time he rode shotgun while I test drove the Tesla.

I begin working on the list of small things to build confidence before I attempt the list of bigger things. I re-evaluate the list every three months to mark things off and add new things. This exercise has helped me expand my knowledge, increase my comfort with failure, and build my confidence to do the big things—like write this book.

Chapter Summary

- Mixed-gender and all-female groups tend to be less hierarchical, more collaborative, and more inclusive to new members joining.

- Women talk more in social and small group settings. Men talk more in public and large group settings where the focus is on providing knowledge or demonstrating skill. In mixed-gender groups, each person has a responsibility to make sure all voices are heard without interruption.

- The pre-meeting before the meeting is an important tool when looking to influence others.

- There is a difference in the amount of confidence that men and women demonstrate in the workplace. Everyone should strive for a realistic self-assessment and demonstrate genuine confidence in their ability. Practice taking risks and doing things outside of your comfort zone to build confidence.

5

Navigating Leader / Employee Relationships

This chapter aims to further summarize the impact of the information presented in the previous chapters and explore the gender-related concerns for each of the following Leader/Employee relationships:

Male Leader / Female Employee
Female Leader / Male Employee
Female Leader / Female Employee
Male Leader / Male Employee

Male Leader / Female Employee - Potential Concerns

- ❖ He may not be aware of her accomplishments because she assumes that her performance speaks for itself, and she does not update him informally like her male peers.

- ❖ He perceives that she is not confident because she exhibits team behavior that lowers her position in the informal hierarchy.

- ❖ He may assume she is not technically strong because she asks a lot of questions compared to her male peers.

- ❖ He might not trust her if she asks him questions in a public forum or talks about him to others.

- ❖ She may worry that he has implied motives when he gives her a deadline (as an opening bid) but doesn't really need it at that time.

- ❖ She may bring options to him to process collaboratively with him, and he may make the decision for her instead.

- ❖ She may vent issues to him, not looking for help but may receive help anyway.

If you are the male leader in this scenario, consider the following:

- ❖ Make sure you are receiving enough communication about the status of projects from the female employee.

Don't rely on her to communicate updates to you informally.

❖ If she brings up options with hopes to collaborate on a decision, ask her which option she is leaning toward and why.

❖ If she comes in to discuss an issue, ask her if she wants your help or if she just wants you to listen.

❖ If it appears that she lacks confidence, reflect on the specific behavior that leads you to that conclusion to determine if she is demonstrating a team player behavior instead.

❖ If she asks questions in a meeting that would be better in a different forum, coach her immediately after the meeting on how to handle that situation better.

❖ Give her specific and detailed developmental feedback tied to business outcomes to help her succeed.

If you are the female employee in this scenario, consider the following:

❖ Communicate frequently (both scheduled and informally) about the work that you are accomplishing. The work doesn't have to be 100% complete; an update on progress is fine.

❖ Be aware of how you ask questions to your leader, especially in front of others. Make sure you do not appear to be challenging his authority in public.

❖ Do not go to your leader to vent issues if you don't want his help to solve your problem. Make sure you are leveraging his time most effectively.

❖ Use peers to collaborate on options to select the best solution instead of your leader.

❖ Do what you said you would, and do not talk about him to others to maintain his trust.

Surprisingly, this scenario is the easiest for most women to navigate in the workplace once they understand the rules of engagement. This is especially true for women who played sports growing up and had male coaches. There is more difficulty in this scenario for the male leader because he is often not aware that women don't understand the rules of engagement. Once the male leader understands this dynamic better and starts giving precise, detailed feedback to the female employee, the environment turns into one that is very effective and rewarding for all involved.

Female Leader / Male Employee - Potential Concerns

❖ She may assume projects are going great, with no issues, because he does not ask for help or escalate problems.

❖ She might not be aware of others he works with on a project because he uses "I" pronouns instead of "we."

❖ She might not trust him because he does not do exactly what he says he will do, or at the time when he says he will do it.

❖ He may conclude she is indecisive because she wants to include more input in her decision making.

❖ He may assume she agrees with him because she nods her head but is surprised when she goes with another idea.

❖ He may not understand the true meaning of feedback or directions because they are given indirectly or with implied meaning.

If you are the female leader in this scenario, consider the following:

❖ Ask the male employee about the challenges he faces on his projects. Look for specific answers.

❖ When discussing a project with a male employee, get clarification on who is working on the project with him.

- ❖ Ask for the appropriate level of input for each decision based on the amount of buy-in needed.

- ❖ Give very clear and specific directions when assigning tasks. Include dates and times of when they should be completed.

- ❖ When listening to male employees discussing a proposal, be aware of your non-verbal head nodding that could imply agreement when there is none.

- ❖ Give him specific and detailed developmental feedback tied to business outcomes to help him succeed.

If you are the male employee in this scenario, consider the following:

- ❖ Don't wait too long before escalating. Some issues can't be resolved at your level.

- ❖ Give the appropriate credit to others that are working with you on a project. Use the "we" pronoun instead of "I" if others are involved in your work.

- ❖ If directions are not specific, don't make assumptions. Ask for clarity on dates and times. She will have a higher level of trust if tasks are completed when she expects them to be completed.

- ❖ If you go to her office and she appears to be bothered about something, ask if it is a good time, or if she would like you to come back another time.

❖ If the feedback received is not clear, be sure to ask for specific examples of behavior to clarify.

Many men find this scenario the most challenging to navigate in the workplace. The things that made them successful in childhood with the sports coach or scout leader don't necessarily work with their female leader. They can sometimes be left unclear about the hierarchy within the team and unclear about how to meet the specific goals and expectations set for them. It may not be as simple to drop in early/late (or go to happy hour) to give her informal updates. If they both focus on frequent, clear communications, they will attain an effective and rewarding working relationship.

Female Leader / Female Employee - Potential Concerns

* ❖ The leader may not be aware of her employee's accomplishments because the employee assumes that her performance speaks for itself.

* ❖ The leader may downplay her authority with the employee, making it difficult for the employee to take direction from her.

* ❖ The employee may see the leader as a friend and be surprised when given direct or difficult performance feedback.

* ❖ The employee may vent too much to the leader.

* ❖ The employee may bring options to the leader to process collaboratively, and the leader may instead make the decision for the employee.

* ❖ The employee may become uncomfortable with the leader because the nature of the relationship makes it difficult to maintain the power dead even.

If you are the female leader in this scenario, consider the following:

* ❖ Don't downplay your authority. Be kind, but don't hesitate to have the difficult conversations. Give detailed developmental feedback to help your employee succeed.

❖ If your employee brings up options hoping to collaborate on a decision, ask her which option she leans toward and why.

❖ If your employee comes in to discuss an issue, ask her if she would like your help or if she just wants you to listen.

❖ Ask for the appropriate level of input for each decision based on the amount of buy-in needed.

❖ Give very clear and specific directions when assigning tasks. Include dates and times of when they should be completed.

❖ Be aware of the natural awkwardness that comes from this dynamic. There is no way to make the power dead even, and that's ok.

If you are the female employee in this scenario, consider the following:

❖ Communicate frequently both formally and informally about the work that you are accomplishing. The work doesn't have to be 100 % complete; an update on progress is fine.

❖ Do not go to your leader to vent issues or share your frustrations; find a peer or trusted friend to confide in instead.

❖ Use peers to collaborate on options to select the best solution rather than going straight to your leader.

❖ If directions are not specific, don't make assumptions. Ask for clarity on dates and times. Your leader will have a higher level of trust with you if tasks are completed when she expects them to be completed.

❖ Be aware of the natural awkwardness that comes from this dynamic. There is no way to make the power dead even, and that's ok.

This scenario is often the most difficult for females in the workplace to navigate because its structure violates the power dead even rule. However, if done effectively, it can be one of the most powerful and rewarding relationships that a female in the workplace can build.

Both the leader and the employee must have the success of each other as a priority for it to work. When women support, mentor, and give each other a hand in the workplace, it creates a highly effective and inclusive business environment.

Male Leader / Male Employee - Potential Concerns

❖ The leader may assume projects are going great and without issues, because the employee is not asking for help or escalating issues.

❖ The leader might not be aware of others he works with on a project because the employee uses "I" pronouns instead of "we."

❖ The leader may conclude the employee is overconfident compared to his performance or not as confident as his peers because he exhibits more team behavior.

❖ The leader might not trust the employee if he asks questions in a public forum or talks about him to others.

❖ The employee may feel like he is not allowed to talk as much in meetings if the leader solicits inputs from everyone.

If you are the male leader in this scenario, consider the following:

❖ Ask the employee about the challenges he is facing on his projects. Look for specific answers.

❖ When discussing projects with your employee, clarify who works on the project with him.

- ❖ If it appears the employee lacks confidence or seems overconfident, reflect on the specific behavior that leads you to that conclusion and determine what is needed to lead him to an honest self-assessment.

- ❖ Facilitate meetings to ensure input from all participants is heard. Watch for the employee talking too much or interrupting others.

- ❖ Give the employee specific and detailed developmental feedback tied to business outcomes in order to help him succeed.

If you are the male employee in this scenario, consider the following:

- ❖ Escalate when needed. Don't wait too long; some issues can't be resolved at your level.

- ❖ Give appropriate credit to others on the team who are working with you on a project. Use the "we" pronoun if others are involved.

- ❖ Be aware of how you ask your leader questions, especially in front of others. Make sure not to appear to be challenging his authority in public.

- ❖ To maintain his trust, do what you said you would do, and do not talk about him to others.

- ❖ Be aware of how much you talk in meetings; don't talk over others or interrupt them.

This scenario is the most straightforward for men to navigate in the workplace. Because of the way most boys are socialized from playing childhood games and sports, they naturally understand that the male leader has assumed the coach or scout leader role and treat him accordingly. It is easier for both the leader and the employee to achieve an effective working relationship because both parties are more likely to be working from the same set of rules.

Gender Spectrum

When discussing these concepts with a male colleague, he shared that his female leader got upset with him when he asked her questions in meetings and did not seem to trust him even though he was completing tasks on time. She was demonstrating behavior more consistent with the male end of the gender spectrum. He realized he needed to adapt his behavior to have a more successful relationship with her.

It is important to treat each person as a unique individual. If you find that your leader is demonstrating behavior that is not what you expect, it is a good indication that you may need to adapt your behavior to what works best for the situation.

Impact at Home

6

DOING LIFE TOGETHER

Just as there are gender communication differences that show up in the workplace, those same differences follow us home and impact our personal relationships.

Trust

The definition of trust discussed in relation to the workplace also applies here. Because women are more likely to share openly with a friend, they must be careful to guard the privacy and trust in their relationships. To maintain trust, men must do what they say they will do at home just as they do at work. To understand the impact this could have, let's explore the effects of broken trust between Kiara and Jayden.

Kiara called out to Jayden as he started out the door. "What time will you get home from work tonight? I will be home around six, and I plan to cook dinner for us. I have some great steaks that need to be used."

"I will be home around six, too. See you later," said Jayden as he walked out the door.

At six, Kiara started cooking dinner. She had everything ready at 6:45, but Jayden was not home, had not texted, and Kiara became worried. She texted him but received no response. Around 7:45, Jayden arrived home.

Kiara met him at the door. "I thought you said you would be home at six?" Her hands were fisted on her hips. "Now, dinner is cold, and these steaks are not going to be good reheated. Where have you been? I texted you!"

Her angry tone surprised Jayden, and he took a step back. "We won a big account at work, so I stopped at happy hour with a few of the guys to celebrate."

"Why didn't you text me and let me know?" Kiara's voice broke. "And I suppose you already ate dinner, too!"

Jayden sighed. "Well, it came up quickly, and I assumed you wouldn't make a big deal about it. I can eat some of what you fixed, too."

"Forget it!" Kiara stormed out of the room.

The next day, Kiara told her best friend Sherri about what happened. A week later, Kiara and Jayden were at an event together, and Sherri was also in attendance. Sherri saw Jayden in a group talking, so she approached him.

"Hey Jayden, are you still in the doghouse? I heard that you totally stood up Kiara's steak dinner last week," Sherri teased.

"She made a bigger deal about it than it was," he said.

On the drive home, Jayden was quiet and scowling. He turned to Kiara and asked, "Why are you telling Sherri all our business?"

"What are you talking about?"

"You told Sherri about our fight last week."

"Yes," Kiara replied. "I mentioned it to her because she could tell I was upset about something. I told her how you ignored a steak dinner to go to happy hour with the guys."

"Well, she brought it up in front a whole group of people at the party," Jayden complained, scowling and gripping the steering wheel tightly.

This example demonstrates a bad cycle relationships can get into when trust is broken. Jayden broke Kiara's trust when he did not come home when he said he would and did not inform her of his change of plans. His actions communicated to Kiara that his work and his buddies were more important to him than the time and effort she put into making dinner.

Kiara broke Jayden's trust when she told Sherri about the situation. Kiara speaking badly about Jayden to Sherri communicated to Jayden that she did not respect him.

Sherri broke Kiara's trust when she brought up the sensitive topic in front of a group of people. When Sherri shared their private conversation with Jayden and others, she communicated to Kiara that she did not value their relationship.

To rebuild trust with Kiara, Jayden needs to apologize to Kiara and show her that he is committed to doing what he says he will do in the future.

To rebuild trust with Jayden, Kiara needs to apologize for sharing their personal details and demonstrate that she will only talk respectfully about him to others going forward.

To rebuild trust with Kiara, Sherri needs to apologize to Kiara and promise not to disclose personal conversations in the future.

When relationships start to break down, it is often because of a broken trust cycle like the scenario above. While each person can justify their actions, the net result is damage to the relationships. Unless the parties in the relationship purposely apologize and modify their behavior, they will not be able to break the cycle, and the relationship will die a death by a thousand cuts.

Hints and Implied Meaning

One of the significant behaviors that could be tied to the gender differences in the brain is *hinting*. Women tend to use hints, indirect comments, to express their wants and needs. This is especially common in personal relationships. As a result, they more readily pick up on the hints of others. Because using hints and indirect communication is such a natural way of communicating for women, they may be incredulous that most men do not pick up on hints as easily as women do—if they pick up on them at all.

Men are straightforward in their communications and tend to say exactly what they mean. In addition, researchers from the

University of Duisburg-Essen in Germany did a study that showed that men also had trouble recognizing emotions in women's eyes. The men were presented with 36 photos of pairs of eyes (18 male and 18 female) and asked to determine the emotional state of the person in the photo. While they were thinking, fMRI images were captured of their brains. The men in the study had more trouble recognizing emotions in female eyes than male eyes. This research concluded that men find it easier to read the emotional cues of other men than from women.

Two weeks before my birthday, I was at my kitchen table with my husband sitting next to me reading his iPad. I noticed over his shoulder that the musical *Wicked* was coming to town the weekend of my birthday. Pointing to the announcement on the screen, I said excitedly, "Oh look, the musical *Wicked* is coming to town in two weeks. I love *Wicked*!"

My husband nodded and continued to read his iPad.

I thought I'd given him an obvious hint as to what I wanted for my birthday and that I would get a great birthday gift. I didn't. We did not go to *Wicked* for my birthday.

I'm sure that the folks on the male end of the spectrum are wondering, "Why didn't you just say you wanted to go to the musical?" That is a very logical thing to ask. Having done a lot of research on this topic, I now know that a direct request would have gotten me tickets to the musical. I considered doing that; however, some part of my brain hoped that if he *really* loved me, he would pick up on my obvious hint.

For the sake of research, I asked him, "What *exactly* went through your mind when I told you that I loved *Wicked* and said it was coming to town?"

My husband thought for a few seconds, then replied "I thought, 'Yep, she loves *Wicked.*'"

"Wow," I replied. "Did it ever cross your mind that I gave you a hint about what I wanted for my birthday?"

He looked as confused as if I'd presented him with a Schrödinger equation. "No."

He did not do what I expected him to do, which was to look at the date of the musical, notice it was my birthday weekend, and buy us tickets. It's clear that I expected his brain to work like mine and make all the connections, which were obvious... to me (and likely to many of the women reading this book).

Successful relationships depend on matched expectations; if we expect one thing to happen, and something entirely different happens, it can cause disappointment and conflict. For women, it helps us to be clear about what we would like to happen, so in this situation, I should have told my husband that I would like to go to *Wicked* for my birthday. For men, if you want to exceed the expectations of a woman, try to pick up on her hints. The more you practice, the better your brain will be at identifying hints. Here are some examples of the common types of hints that women give.

- If you are walking at the mall, and she points to a window display and says, "Oh, I love that purse!" or

"Isn't that a pretty necklace?" She just gave you a clue as to a possible gift you can get her in the near future.

- If you are at a bonfire, and she leans over and says, "It's cold out here." That is not just a statement about the weather; she expects a response. She either wants her date to offer a coat, or she wants to go inside, or she may be ready to leave entirely. A response like, "Do you want my coat, or would you like to go back inside?" would be appropriate.

- If she is uncharacteristically silent, she may be giving you a hint that she is mad or upset about something. An appropriate response would be, "You seem quiet," followed by sitting next to her with an arm around her shoulder. Her reaction to that gesture should tell you if she is mad at you, mad at the world, or just sad. Be patient, and don't rush her to speak.

Memory and Mental Replays

Because women's brains are always trying to connect data points, it is common for women to perform mental replays of situations in their heads, like an instant replay at a sports game. They replay the dialogue, and non-verbal cues over and over in their brains to pick up on connections, nuances, and to analyze if the situation could have been handled better.

As a result, women have an incredible ability to remember details, dates, events, dialogue, and emotional reactions. Men, however, do not do as many of these types of replays, and as a result, they tend not to remember events in such vivid detail.

For example, a man and a woman attend a party together. They socialize with other couples throughout the night, and at the end of the evening, the woman describes, verbatim, several conversations, and her emotions attached to each of those conversations. Men are often surprised that women can remember the events of the evening in such vivid detail.

Men also may forget a detail from a significant event (like what song was playing on their first date), and women interpret this as not caring about the event. This is an area where women can extend a little grace to the men in their lives for not remembering all the details, and remember that men's brains do not facilitate remembering the details as easily as women's brains.

In 2011, Daniel Johnson and Mark Whisman conducted a study which confirmed that women "ruminate" more than men. The word ruminate has two meanings: one is the think deeply, and the other is to chew the cud, like a cow. This implies worrying about something repeatedly.

On occasion, this replay process can turn into full-blown anxiety if she cannot stop the replay cycle. It is very important to recognize when our brains are in a replay or rumination cycle and kick the thought processing into a different area.

The most helpful activities are those where the brain cannot both process the replay and do the activity at the same time. If you are in your car, you can try singing out loud, listening to (and following the plot of) an audiobook, prayer, or talking on the phone about a different topic. If you are not confined to your car, you can try exercising outside or going to the greeting card section of a nearby store and reading funny greeting cards.

The 2018 HSOA *Journal of Psychiatry, Depression & Anxiety* stated that women are more likely than men to be diagnosed with an anxiety disorder during their lifetime, and the tendency to ruminate plays a role in that.

Many people are familiar with the Big 5 Personality test that analyzes people across five dimensions of personality (Openness, Conscientiousness, Agreeableness, Extraversion, and Neuroticism). The Big 5 test is one of the only personality tests that specifically calls out neuroticism, which relays levels of anxiety, the ability to deal with stress, and the ability to maintain calmness under pressure. Based on the gender difference in anxiety mentioned above, one would expect to see differences in the way men and women score in the Big 5 personality neuroticism results. In 2017, Sergei Shchebetenko conducted a study that confirmed that women scored higher than men in neuroticism, which was the only area of gender difference in the Big 5 personality traits that was not easily explained by other factors.

If a female scores low on the neuroticism scale on the Big 5, does that mean she does not use mental replays? While there is no specific research on that topic, I will give an example from my personal experience.

I scored lower than the average female on neuroticism on the Big 5 test. However, after I deal with a difficult personal or work situation, I often find myself ruminating on it. The repetitive replays overtake my thoughts, and I get stuck in a mental loop trying to determine what I can do to make it better. After several cycles, I notice that I am starting to obsess about it, and at that point, I make a conscious decision to try to kick myself out of the cycle. I suspect the awareness that I am ruminating happens because I am lower on the neuroticism scale. That said, one data point is not a scientific study. My theory is that the lower the person is on the neuroticism scale, the less likely they are to replay and get stuck in a rumination cycle.

If you suffer from anxiety, the types of techniques described above may help to alleviate the anxiety. Each person is unique; what works for one person may not work for another.

Asking for Help

Asking for directions or help is a gender difference that is widely discussed in popular culture. Most people have heard the stereotype that men prefer not to stop and ask for directions or read the instruction manual when assembling things, and it's a stereotype for a reason. *Gadget Helpline* analyzed 75,000 calls to their technical support line and found that 64% of men and 24% of women had not read the instruction booklet that came with their consumer electronic device before calling for help. Our preference for how to accomplish a task can be a source of conflict in relationships.

Two of the most seemingly benign, yet stressful, things that I have ever done with my husband were assembling a swing set (there were literally 50+ screws left over) and canoeing an unknown river together (we ended up wedged on top of a rock). Both activities included facing unknown challenges with no assigned leader and a possibility of assigning blame if things didn't go so well. Both personality and gender differences can make a challenging task even more difficult. Here are a few hints for navigating these types of relationship land mines:

- Discuss roles and processes before you begin the task (who will do each task, will written instructions be used, etc.). This small step can make a big difference in the shared experience!

- If things become stressful, take a break and remove yourself from the situation for a while, if possible. (We stopped in a cove and took a little swim after the "stuck on a rock" incident.)

- Don't assign blame or escalate an argument. Remember that you are on the same team.

- If all else fails, remove yourself from the situation entirely (pay for someone else to assemble, get out of the boat, etc.).

Giving Directions and Nagging

As mentioned earlier, women tend to be more indirect in their communications when assigning tasks to others. Let's consider these requests to take the garbage outside.

Indirect: The garbage is starting to stink.

Indirect: When are you going to take out that garbage?

Direct: Take out that stinky garbage today!

What often happens is the first and second bids are given indirectly, but the third request becomes significantly more direct.

This brings us to the topic of nagging, which is defined as asking for something to be done repeatedly. This behavior can be very detrimental to relationships because it is negative for both the giver and the receiver.

Even though much progress has been made over the years in sharing the household chores, a 2017 study of heterosexual couples at William Patterson University and Columbia Business School showed that women still tend to do more of the housework and more of the reminding of others in the home to complete their tasks. Repetitive reminders can lead to nagging. Here are a few tips if you find yourself in a cycle of constant reminding:

- Give very clear instructions on what needs to be done.

- No critiquing: if you want something done a certain way, do it yourself.

- Don't insist that a task be done on your schedule; be patient.

- Remind your partner that it is better to decline a task than to break a promise.

- Do the task for a loved one as an act of kindness.

The last tip may seem counterintuitive. After all, they may have done nothing to deserve your kindness. My husband makes a peanut butter and jelly sandwich every day, and every day he leaves sticky stuff on the counter. It turns out that sticky stuff on the counter is a pet peeve I didn't know I had until I got married. I nagged him about wiping the counters for *years*. I couldn't understand why he wouldn't do this small thing for me. It started to affect our relationship and make me quicker to anger about many other things.

One day, as I read a relationship article, it recommended that I should do one unselfish thing for my partner every day to improve my relationship. I decided that wiping the counter would be my act of love, and I didn't mention it to anyone.

In the beginning, I thought he would notice and would be appreciative, but he didn't. What *did* happen was, over time, something changed inside me. I realized that it took less than thirty seconds to wipe the counters, and everyone was happier. I was not angry, and as a result, I nagged him less. I decided to accept his behavior as one of the quirks of the person that I married and move on.

In a study of 373 couples conducted at Oakland University, Dr. Terri Orbuch found that, instead of only focusing on fixing what is wrong in relationships, couples are happier when they add positive behaviors to the relationship. She recommends doing small acts of kindness daily, providing affirmation, compliments, help, support, and encouragement. When a partner makes us feel loved and supported, we are much more willing to forgive when they make mistakes.

Relationship Building

For over 40 years, Dr. John Gottman has been conducting research on heterosexual and same-sex relationships, marriage, and divorce. He and his wife, Dr. Julie Gottman, created the Gottman Institute and the Gottman Method of couples' therapy with the goal of helping couples create and maintain greater love and health in relationships.

In the book *The Seven Principles for Making Marriage Work*, Dr. John Gottman describes the reasons (based on his research data) that marriages succeed. The studies included three groups of couples: 1) couples that divorced 2) couples that stayed together and were happy, and 3) couples that stayed together and were unhappy. Based on these studies, Dr. Gottman pinpointed seven principles that all successful relationships shared. The happy couples in his research did the following:

1. Built Love Maps

   Started from a base of friendship, they longed to know each other deeply. They built Love Maps, which include all the relevant information about their partner's life; their inner psychological world, history, worries, stresses, joys, and hopes.

2. Shared Fondness and Admiration

   They showed fondness, admiration, and appreciation to each other. Each partner felt that the person they married was worthy of honor and respect.

3. Turned Towards Instead of Away

   Couples stated their needs and were aware of bids for connection and responded to them. They used small moments of everyday life as the building blocks of relationship. They demonstrated fondness in seemingly mundane gestures, thus increasing the sense of positivity toward each other.

4. Let Their Partner Influence Them

   Couples shared power, listened to each other, and were open to compromise and changing their opinions.

5. Managed Conflict

   "Managed" conflict rather than "resolved" conflict—raised issues calmly without a harsh tone. They learned to make and accept repair attempts and were tolerant of their partner's faults.

6. Overcame Gridlock

   They created an atmosphere that encouraged each person to talk honestly about his or her hopes, values, convictions, and aspirations. They recognized that gridlock is a sign that dreams aren't being addressed or respected.

7. Created Shared Meaning

   Couples developed a shared culture that reflected the unique values, history, customs, rituals, and connection within the relationship.

There were two areas in Dr. Gottman's research, where he discovered gender differences that influenced the above principles. The first area was principle number four, Let Their Partner Influence Them. His research found that in heterosexual marriages where the husband resists sharing power with his wife, the marriage is four times more likely to end in divorce, or drone on unhappily, than marriages where the husband shared power.

The second area was in principle number five, Manage Conflict. Dr. Gottman found that most of the time, women are the ones to bring up difficult relationship issues and tend to use a harsh tone when starting those conversations.

There is an interesting interplay between these two areas. If the husband listens to his wife and allows her to influence him, she, in turn, will be less likely to be harsh when raising issues.

In his book, Dr. Gottman shares exercises that couples can do to evaluate their relationship in each of the seven principle areas. His resources, methods, and therapy are backed by extensive research and are highly recommended for those who want to dig deeper into ways to strengthen relationships (www.Gottman.com).

Adapting

Adapting is intentionally changing our behavior to improve our lives and relationships.

My husband and I have adapted our behavior as a result of better understanding the gender differences and where we each land on the gender spectrum.

For me, I have intentionally adapted to give very specific directions. I don't rely on implied meaning. I also avoid talking about my husband in a negative way, even when he is not there to hear it. I try to be kinder than necessary and forgive quickly.

My husband has also adapted his behavior. When I come to him with an issue, he will always ask if I want his help to fix it or if I just want him to listen. He also is very trustworthy about doing what he says he will do. If he is going to arrive home later than expected, he will text and let me know.

We are both clear about the things we will do and those things we won't. If either of us commits to doing something, we will complete it. When asked to do something around the house, we can say "no," and that answer is acceptable. It's better to know what not to expect so that we can make other arrangements.

These seemingly minor changes to our behavior have made a significant impact on the success of our relationship. Of course, like all relationships, ours is not perfect. It takes intentional effort for us to relate meaningfully to each other in the seven principle areas that are shared in Dr. Gottman's book.

Chapter Summary

- Both genders maintain trust by keeping their commitments and protecting the privacy of the relationship.

- Women tend to use more hints than men and readily pick up on the hints of others. Men are very straightforward in their communications and tend to say exactly what they mean.

- Because women's brains are always trying to connect data points, women tend to perform mental replays more than men. If the mental replays get stuck in a rumination cycle, anxiety increases.

- Men tend to give directions directly; women tend to use indirect methods. Women tend to do more of the housework and more of the task reminders to others in the home.

- Dr. Gottman's research explains seven principles that help couples navigate their relationships and stay together.

- To strengthen relationships, it is important to adapt our behavior to the unique needs of the individuals and understand where they are on the gender spectrum.

7

INTERACTING WITH OTHERS

Listening

As mentioned earlier, women openly share their complaints and concerns to connect with a friend or partner. When a woman shares a concern, the response she expects is an acknowledgment *"Wow, that is a really tough situation."* or commiseration *"Yes, I have experienced that exact same thing!"*. Most times, she is not looking for solutions to the problem.

If her partner is male, he may interpret this sharing as her asking for help and try to fix the issue, even if she was not looking for help. If this is something that has been shared before or is a chronic situation (for example, she hates her job or she's dealing with an ongoing family situation), it can be particularly frustrating for her partner to just listen and not offer solutions.

York University psychologist Faye Doell conducted a study that showed that there are two types of listening: "listening to understand" and "listening to respond." Those who "listen to understand" have greater satisfaction in their interpersonal relationships.

So, how do we know if we are listening to understand or to respond? When we are listening to understand, we pay attention to what is said without distraction. We suspend judgment about the thoughts and feelings that are shared with us. We don't interrupt. We don't let our minds wander. We ask clarifying questions and repeat what we hear for confirmation. And most importantly of all, *we don't plan what we are going to say in response*. This is not an easy skill for either gender to master, but it is a very powerful tool to improve relationships.

Humor

When looking for a relationship, both genders say they want someone with a sense of humor. A 2006 study published in the *Journal of Evolution and Human Behavior* found that women interpreted this as "someone who makes me laugh," and men interpreted as "someone who laughs at my jokes." The study asked 127 subjects to choose potential partners for either a one-night stand, a date, a short-term relationship, a long-term relationship, or friendship. In every context other than friendship, men preferred women who laughed at their jokes to those who made their own jokes. Women, however, preferred partners who made them laugh.

One of the preferred methods of humor among men is teasing, name-calling, and mock attacks. Remember the way Jack invited me to play the video game in the earlier example? He said he could "kick my ass," and his tone was one of playful banter. It's also common for men to call other men by nicknames and to have a conversation like this:

Jack looked at George and asked, "Who is coming to lunch with us?"

George replied, "I know Shorty and Stinkweed are coming, but Robo said he'd be late."

John Morreal, a humor expert at the College of William and Mary, has studied humor for twenty-five years. He explains, "Men taunt other men with clever nicknames and insults, that isn't something that women do. They don't tend to play practical jokes or engage in humor that humiliates or puts somebody down."

The most common form of humor among women, however, is self-mocking. Women tend to make jokes at their own expense, describing their latest foible or thing they did that they found funny. They use humor as another way to form connections.

Having spent most of my life in male-dominated environments, I am used to the male form of humor. I occasionally participate in it, but only if no other women are participating.

A woman can tell when she has become an accepted part of an all-male team when they start teasing her and calling her names. One male coworker (and good friend) affectionately called me "Little Shit" and I referred to him as "Big Jerk." While many women will accept this behavior and participate, most will admit that they find it uncomfortable and not their authentic style.

A 2006 study published in the *Journal of Pragmatics*, found that men use a teasing style of humor more within an all-male group than in a mixed group. They also found that women use more self-targeting humor with an all-female group. In a mixed group, women increase the amount of teasing-style humor but will typically tease only the male members of the group, not the other females.

Women may take it personally if another woman calls them names or attempts male-styled mock attacks. This is especially true if the women are merely acquaintances and not close friends or family.

Understanding the humor style differences of others may make us more accepting of different styles of humor. Shared laughter and humor are important building blocks to strong friendships and relationships.

Negotiation

When it comes to negotiation, men and women may have slightly different approaches, but ultimately end up with the same results. Men typically start with the first bid, while women start with a question. To demonstrate this concept, consider these example negotiations:

Barbara approached Sally, "What day works best for your schedule to go to lunch next week?"

Sally checked her phone and replied, "I'm open on Tuesday or Friday."

"Ok, let's make it Friday at noon."

This time, let's look at the same negotiation but with two men:

George walked over to Suresh and asked, "Are you open next Wednesday at noon for lunch?"

"No, but I am open on Friday."

"Ok, let's make it Friday at noon," George confirmed.

Negotiations show up in all kinds of ways in our lives. For example, my husband is a teacher and likes to go to yard sales to find things for his classroom. We often find multiple things at a yard sale that we want to purchase, and we each approach the seller differently with several items in our hands.

I approached the payment table and asked, "What deal can you give me if I bundle all these purchases together?"

The seller replied, "How about $15.00 for everything?"

Now, contrast that to my husband's approach:

My husband approached the seller, "Will you take $15.00 for all these items?"

The seller replied, "Yes, that will work."

The success of these negotiations at yard sales may depend on the gender of the seller. I have found that if the seller is male, then opening with a first bid works best. If the seller is female, then opening with a question works best. I observed my husband approach a female seller and ask if she would take $15.00 for a bunch of items. She visibly flinched, then frantically went through the items to do the math to determine if the deal was acceptable for her. It was clear that this made her uncomfortable.

When negotiating at yard sales or online marketplaces, it is always helpful to strike up a conversation with the seller, act friendly, and see if they will give any clues as to why they are selling and how badly they want to sell their items. It's also helpful to observe how open they are to others that try to negotiate with them. Show kindness, and don't bid too low, which they may find insulting.

Decision Making

A classic way that decision making comes up in our personal lives is deciding where to grab dinner.

On my way home from work last Friday night, my husband called and asked. "Where do you want to go for dinner?"

"I don't care. Where do you want to go?" I'd had a long day, was suffering from a little decision fatigue, and wasn't expecting to have to make a decision again.

"How about Chinese food?"

"No," I answered, "I had that recently for lunch."

My husband pauses, sorts through restaurant options mentally, then offers, "How about the Mexican grill?"

"Hmm… I'm not in the mood for Mexican."

My husband sighed, and his voice raised slightly as he demanded, "What *are* you in the mood for?"

"I don't know." I really didn't. "Give me some more options, and I will see which one jumps out to me."

"I just gave you two options," I could practically feel his annoyance through the phone's speaker. "I don't want to keep guessing."

"Fine. Let's just stay home." I was equally as angry that I felt like I had to come up with a choice on the spot.

Reflecting on the differences highlighted in the example above, you can see how my husband tried to simply complete a goal (to eat dinner), while I tried to discuss the merits of each option and discover the best option together—bids versus questions. The approach is different, but there is a clearly understood shared goal (to eat dinner). One thing that can bridge the different approaches is to start out with two or three options, then work from there. Let's reimagine how the conversation from earlier *could* have gone, keeping in mind what we've discussed.

"Where do you want to go for dinner?"

It was after six, and we were both hungry, so I knew my husband was looking for a quick answer. I wasn't sure exactly what I wanted, so I threw out a few options. "How about either Thai, steak or pizza. Which sounds good to you?"

"Steak," he chose.

"Ok, let's pick a steakhouse that has a great salad, too."

He breathed a sigh of relief and said, "Ok, let's go to that new steakhouse by the river. I hear their salads are great."

This eliminates unlimited choices, which can drive frustration and allows specific choices as a starting point. Either party can offer the three choices.

Team Dynamic

Children's sports coaches and Scout troop leaders have a significant influence on the children they lead, and many helpful moms and dads volunteer to coach their children's troops and teams. Awareness of gender differences is just as important for coaches as it is for leaders in the workplace.

My husband is a middle school girls volleyball coach. Early in his coaching career, he came in the house and plopped down, sighed heavily, and said, "I made the volleyball girls cry today…again."

Initially, this did not strike me as unusual for middle school girls, but since I was aware of the gender differences, I decided to dig a little deeper. "Tell me *exactly* what happened right before the girls started crying."

He recounted the evening's events. "In a time-out huddle during a close volleyball match, I told the team to pass the ball to Lexi, the best hitter on the floor, so she could spike it. I told Lexi, 'The whole team is relying on you to get the kill so we can win the game.' Then she got a strange look on her face, and the other girls got very uncomfortable in the huddle. They went back out on the volleyball court, Lexi missed the spike, and they lost the game. Every one of the girls' faces got red, and some of them cried and ran into the locker room. They were probably mad because they lost the game."

"Why did you do *that*?" I almost yelled in horror for poor Lexi.

"Do *what*?" he replied, utterly baffled.

"Tell Lexi it was all up to her and single her out in front of the whole team!"

"Because it *was* all up to her!" he threw his hands up in the air.

"Yes, but you didn't have to *tell* her that, especially in front of the team."

The coaching technique that my husband used with the girls is very common in men's sports. It's normal for the pro basketball coach to direct the players to pass the ball to LeBron James for the last basketball shot before the buzzer. It makes very clear the hierarchy, and all the male players are comfortable with following those rules. This does not work as well when dealing with young girls. By singling out the one player, my husband unknowingly violated the power dead even rule, and all the girls got uncomfortable. As a result, the best hitter was overwhelmed with pressure and did not perform well, and they lost the game.

I encouraged him to try an experiment with his team the next season. In addition to the normal skills practice, I told him to add team-building events and to put the focus on the team rather than individuals. He added summer events where they did not touch a volleyball; instead, they went swimming, canoeing, and worked at charities to build relationships.

During the games, instead of saying, "Pass the ball to Lexi, so she can spike it," he would instead say, "Our team plays best when we set the middle position." (The middle position is Lexi's position.) The team responded well to modified coaching. At the end of that season, the team won the District Championship, and he realized that his experiment worked. The team cried less (but let's face it, they were middle-school girls so there was still a little crying), built real friendships, and they won a big trophy! Since that time, he has continued to coach the girls' team, and his focus on teambuilding has been key to building one of the top middle school volleyball programs in the region.

Both men and women can be very competitive and like to win, but the style of coaching that works best on a team may vary if the team is made up of all females or all males.

In a study published in the *International Sport Coaching Journal* in 2016, researcher Leanne Norman concluded that male and female athletes have different needs, and the coaches need to be more "gender-responsive" to build the highest performing teams. They recommended that coaches receive training specific to their team's gender to better understand the motivations and communication styles of the athletes.

Similarly, if a man is leading a girl scout troop or a woman is leading a boy scout troop, they also need to be gender-responsive and understand how to motivate the children in their troops.

Chapter Summary

- Women share concerns looking for connection and someone to listen. Men may interpret this as asking for help and try to fix the issue. Listening to understand is a powerful tool to help all types of relationships.

- Humor is important to relationships. Women are attracted to someone who makes them laugh, and men are attracted to someone that laughs at their jokes. Men use nicknames and mock-attack style humor in their friendships more than women. Women tend to use self-deprecating humor.

- Men and women may have slightly different approaches when negotiating, but ultimately end up with the same results. Men typically start with the first bid, and women start with a question.

- When making decisions, women prefer to sort through the options together. It is best to pick two or three choices as a starting point for the decision.

- The gender differences in the team dynamic show up in sports and scouting as well as workplaces. Coaches and leaders need to be more "gender-responsive" to achieve the highest performance from their teams.

CONCLUSION

As this book draws to a close, my hope is that you now see the world through a new set of goggles. We have explored research on childhood games, hierarchy, and brain science. We have tuned our ears to conversations and reflected on experiences that demonstrate gender communication differences. I have shared advice from the experts and from my personal life experiences.

In the workplace, we explored the impact of gender communication differences on how our performance is perceived as well as our ability to compete for promotions. We looked at how the genders work together, manage conflict, and the different types of behaviors that happen in meetings and groups.

In the home, we discussed the gender behaviors that can cause conflict in personal relationships and reviewed suggestions for small adaptations that can improve relationships in a big way. We also looked at the differences in each gender interaction style and the impact on relationships, friendships, and coaching.

Now that you are equipped to identify the differences, I challenge you to explore them in your own life. Be kind, and be intentional.

See if you can observe the behaviors highlighted in this book and reflect on any changes necessary so that you can get that promotion, strengthen your relationships, and love graciously.

Because we have covered many areas in this book, I have created a summary chart that highlights some of the key differences in communication style between men and women. This chart will act as a helpful guide and memory jogger for you in the future. I have also included a list of frequently asked questions about gender that I received over the years but did not cover directly in this book.

Area	Men	Women
Team Environment	Hierarchy – one up	Team – "power dead even"
In a Group	Banter; will stop talking	Inclusive environment
Dealing with Leader	Self-promote; compliment	Performance speaks for itself
Learning style	Self-study	Asks questions
Trust	Do what you commit + respect	Do what you commit
Conflict	Open arguing; then friendly	May take personally
Decision Making	Less input	More input; collaborate options
Sharing Feelings	Reserved; will show anger	Openly shares to connect
Influence	Meeting before meeting	In meeting
High stakes question	Best guess	Will admit they don't know
Giving Direction	Direct; no implied meaning	Indirect; gives hints
Asking for direction	Delays as long as possible	Asks for help as needed
Humor	Teasing; nicknames	Self-mocking
Negotiation	Opens with first demand	Opens with question

**Chart describes each end of gender spectrum based on research; however, every individual is unique.

FREQUENTLY ASKED QUESTIONS

1. **What impact does identifying in the LGBTQ community have on the gender differences?**

   There is a spectrum of gender behavior, and some identify on more of the male end of the spectrum and some on the female end. LGBTQ individuals are no different in this regard. This is one of the many variables that contribute to our unique position on the gender spectrum.

2. **What about adults that didn't have the traditional types of childhoods that are described in the book?**

   The way we were socialized as children can impact our behavior as adults. Even if we did not play traditional children's games, our experiences helped shape our position on the gender spectrum.

3. **It seems that women talk more about gender communication differences than men. What drives this?**

   While gender differences impact both men and women's lives equally, research shows that women tend to bring up more of the difficult issues in relationships, which makes them more likely to seek solutions to the gender differences they are experiencing.

4. **My boss told me that I need to be more confident. What, specifically, do I need to do**?

It is important to understand what behavior your leader is identifying that makes you appear less confident. You will need to ask them to describe what it looks like when you appear less confident and what specific confident behavior they would expect to see in that situation. There are many aspects to confidence: physical, voice volume, non-verbal cues, active vs. passive language, etc. I highly recommend reading the book *The Confidence Code* by Katty Kay and Claire Shipman.

5. **Do I need a mentor or a sponsor at work**? **How do I get one? Does gender matter?**

You need both mentors and sponsors, and sometimes one person can serve both roles. A mentor is someone who helps coach you on specific actions or career tactics. A sponsor is someone that will put their reputation on the line to recommend you for a promotion. It's unlikely that someone will sponsor you if they don't already know you well. If you have a strong mentor, you can have an honest discussion with them about what it would take to move them from a mentor to a sponsor. The gender of your mentors does not matter. Many people find it helpful to have both male and female mentors.

6. **What is the best way to make sure the leadership team at my company is informed on the gender differences**?

    Talk with a diversity leader or HR person to see if there are training or presentations planned to educate leaders on gender diversity. Also, if you have affinity groups at your company, they can be leveraged to provide educational sessions. It's also a good topic to bring up with a mentor because they may have an awareness of other resources that can be leveraged.

    If you have other questions, please reach out—I would love to hear from you!

    Email to gendergoggles@gmail.com

    https://www.facebook.com/GenderGoggles

    https://www.instagram.com/gendergoggles/

ACKNOWLEDGMENTS

I would like to thank a few of the people who helped me make this book a reality:

To my husband, Mark, you are my encourager, proofreader, and such a good sport about the examples in the book that include you. I am very blessed to share my life with you!

To my children and their spouses, Stephanie and Jeff, Jeremy and Rachel. You guys have cheered me on since the day I mentioned I wanted to write a book. I am so proud of all of you and appreciate your love and support!

To my parents, you gave me roots and wings! You have always encouraged me to follow my dreams!

To "Bob" who was my team leader, coach, and mentor for many years, and today is a valued friend. Thank You! I would not have succeeded without your help!

To my editor, Kate Johnson, thanks for your guidance, feedback, funny stories, and encouragement! You rock!

To the many friends that read the early versions of the book and/or checked in with me regularly, Thank you. You have no idea how much your small gestures of encouragement meant to me and kept me moving forward!

SHARE YOUR FEEDBACK!

Thank you for reading this book!

What are your thoughts? Did you recognize any of the scenarios from your own experience?

I believe that authentic feedback is a gift. If you have found benefit in reading this book, I hope you will take a few minutes and leave me a helpful and detailed review.

Thank you!

Jill
gendergoggles@gmail.com
https://www.facebook.com/GenderGoggles
https://www.instagram.com/gendergoggles/

ABOUT THE AUTHOR

Jill Eaton has worked in Information Technology at Fortune 500 Companies for the last 34 years. She started her career as a programmer and worked her way up to an Executive position. She has a passion for developing talent and led a global Leadership Development Program for ten years. She remains a career coach and mentor to many.

Jill was a featured presenter on the topic of gender communication differences at companies, universities, and conferences.

In her spare time, she loves to cook (and eat!), travel, and read.

Jill is based in Louisville, KY, where she resides with her husband and pets.

NOTES

References and citations are organized by topic and page number. I recognize that scientific literature changes over time, and references may need to be updated.

Impact of Childhood Games

- 6 Pellegrini, A. D., Kato, K., Blatchford, P., & Baines, E. (2002). A Short-term longitudinal study of children's playground games across the first year of school: implications for social competence and adjustment to school. *American Educational Research Journal, 39*(4), 991-1015. doi:10.3102/00028312039004991
- 7 Tannen, D. (2010, June). He said, she said. *Scientific American Mind*. 54-59.

Hierarchy and Power

- 9 Heim, P., Hughes, T., & Golant, S. K. (2015). *Hardball for women: winning at the game of business.* (3rd ed.). Plume.

Brain Science

- 12 Zaidi, Z. F. (2010). Gender differences in human brain: a review. *The Open Anatomy Journal, 2*, 37-55. doi:10.2174/1877609401002010037
- 12 Ingalhalikar, M., Smith, A., Parker, D., Satterthwaite, T. D., Elliott, M. A., Ruparel, K., Hakonarson, H., Gur, R. E., Gur, R. C., & Verma, R. (2013). Sex differences in the structural connectome of the human brain. Proceedings of the National Academy of Sciences, 111(2), 823–828. https://doi.org/10.1073/pnas.1316909110
- 13 Brain Connectivity Study Reveals Striking Differences Between Men and Women. (2013, February 12). [Press release]. *Penn Medicine.* https://www.pennmedicine.org/news/news-releases/2013/december/brain-connectivity-study-revea
- 13 Farrel, B., & Farrel, P. (2016). *Men are like waffles, women are like spaghetti.* Harvest House.

Performance and Promotion

- 19 Women in the workplace 2019: (2019, October 23). McKinsey & Company & Lean In. https://wearethecity.com/women-in-the-workplace-2019-mckinsey-company-lean-in/

Promoting Accomplishments

- 20 Kessler, C. (2019, December 19). Why don't women self-promote as much as men? *Harvard Business Review.* https://hbr.org/2019/12/why-dont-women-self-promote-as-much-as-men

Feedback

- 25 Correll, S. J.& Simard, C. (2016, April 29). Research: vague feedback is holding women back. *Harvard Business Review.* https://hbr.org/2016/04/research-vague-feedback-is-holding-women-back
- 25 Heilman, M. E. (2012). Gender stereotypes and workplace bias. *Research in Organizational Behavior, 32*, 113-135. doi:10.1016/j.riob.2012.11.003

Sharing Emotions

- 29 Heim, P., Hughes, T., & Golant, S. K. (2015). *Hardball for women: winning at the game of business.* (3rd ed.). Plume.
- 29 Simpkin, T. (2020, January 8). Mixed feelings: How to deal with emotions at work. *Totaljobs.* https://www.totaljobs.com/advice/emotions-at-work
- 31 Wilding, M. (2018, June 15). The surprising truth about crying at work. *Forbes.* https://www.forbes.com/sites/melodywilding/2018/06/11/the-surprising-truth-about-crying-at-work/

Asking Questions

- 33 Weingarten, E. (2019, June 19). Who asks questions, and what it tells us. *Behavioral Scientist.* https://behavioralscientist.org/who-asks-questions-and-what-it-tells-us/
- 33 Rosette, A. S., Mueller, J. S., & Lebel, R. D. (2015). Are male leaders penalized for seeking help? The influence of gender and asking behaviors on competence perceptions. *The Leadership Quarterly, 26*(5), 749-762. doi:10.1016/j.leaqua.2015.02.001

Decision Making and Giving Directions

- 36 Gernreich, C., & Exner, C. (2015). A comparison of the influence of gender on managerial decision making. Thesis. Technische Universität Carolo-Wilhelmina zu Braunschweig. https://www.researchgate.net/publication/278679030_A_Comparison_of_the_Influence_of_Gender_on_Managerial_Decision_Making
- 37 Lane, S. D. (2016). *Interpersonal communication: competence and contexts* (p. 198). Routledge/Taylor & Francis.

Trust (At Work)

- 41 Heim, P., Hughes, T., & Golant, S. K. (2015). *Hardball for women: winning at the game of business.* (3rd ed.). Plume.

Conflict

- 45 Reuell, P. (2019, September 12). Resolving conflict: men vs. women. *The Harvard Gazette.* https://news.harvard.edu/gazette/story/2016/08/resolving-conflict-men-vs-women/

Non Verbal Cues

- 49 Lafrance, M., & Vial, A. C. (2016). Gender and nonverbal behavior. *APA Handbook of Nonverbal Communication.,* 139-161. doi:10.1037/14669-006
- 51 Nelson, A. (2014, April 27). Why you stand side-by-side or face-to-face. *Psychology Today.* https://www.psychologytoday.com/us/blog/he-speaks-she-speaks/201404/why-you-stand-side-side-or-face-face

Group Dynamics

- 55 Carli, L. L. (2009). Gender and group behavior. *Handbook of Gender Research in Psychology,* 337-358. doi:10.1007/978-1-4419-1467-5_14

Talking in Meetings

- 56 Karpowitz, C. F., Mendelberg, T., & Shaker, L. (2012). Gender inequality in deliberative participation. *American Political Science Review, 106*(3), 533-547. doi:10.1017/s0003055412000329

- 56 Hancock, A. B., & Rubin, B. A. (2014). Influence of communication partner's gender on language. *Journal of Language and Social Psychology, 34*(1), 46-64. doi:10.1177/0261927x14533197
- 57 Maxfield, D., Grenny, J., & McMillan, C. (2018*). Emotional inequality: solutions for women in the workplace.* VitalSmarts. https://www.vitalsmarts.fr/wp-content/uploads/2018/08/Women_in_the_Workplace_eBook.pdf

Mansplaining

- 58 Merriam-Webster. (n.d.) Mansplaining. In Merriam-Webster Dictionary. Retrieved August 15, 2020 from https://www.merriam-webster.com/dictionary/mansplaining
- 58 Solnit, R. (2014). Men explain things to me. In *Men explain things to me: and other essays*. Granta.
- 58 Goodwin, K. (2018). Mansplaining, explained in one simple chart. BBC *Worklife*. https://www.bbc.com/worklife/article/20180727-mansplaining-explained-in-one-chart

Influence

- 62 Flynn, K., Flynn, J., & Holt, M. D. (2014, June). Success on the corporate stage: why meetings matter even more for women. Flynn Heath Holt Leadership. https://flynnheath.com/wp-content/uploads/2016/01/Why-

Meetings-Matter-Even-More-for-Women_FHH-
Report_June-2014.pdf

Honesty and Confidence

- 64 Reuben, E., Sapienza, P., & Zingales, L. (2014). How stereotypes impair women's careers in science. *Proceedings of the National Academy of Sciences, 111*(12), 4403-4408. doi:10.1073/pnas.1314788111
- 64 Ehrlinger, J., & Dunning, D. (2003). How chronic self-views influence (and potentially mislead) estimates of performance. *Journal of Personality and Social Psychology, 84*(1), 5-17. doi:10.1037/0022-3514.84.1.5
- 65 Anderson, C., Brion, S., Moore, D. A., & Kennedy, J. A. (2012). A status-enhancement account of overconfidence. *Journal of Personality and Social Psychology, 103*(4), 718-735. doi:10.1037/a0029395
- 65 Moore, D. (2018, January 22). Overconfidence. *Psychology Today.* https://www.psychologytoday.com/us/blog/perfectly-confident/201801/overconfidence
- 66 Kay, K., & Shipman, C. (2018). *The confidence code: The science and art of self-assurance-- what women should know.* HarperBusiness.

Hints and Implied Meaning

- 89 Schiffer, B., Pawliczek, C., Müller, B. W., Gizewski, E.
  R., & Walter, H. (2013). Why don't men understand women?
  altered neural networks for reading the language of male and
  female eyes. *PLoS ONE, 8*(4).
  doi:10.1371/journal.pone.0060278

Memory and Mental Replays

- 92 Johnson, D. P., & Whisman, M. A. (2013). Gender
  differences in rumination: A meta-analysis. *Personality and
  Individual Differences, 55*(4), 367-374.
  doi:10.1016/j.paid.2013.03.019
- 93 Jalnapurkar, I., Allen, M., & Pigott, T. (2018). Sex
  differences in anxiety disorders: a review. *Psychiatry,
  Depression & Anxiety, 4*, 1-9. doi:10.24966/pda-0150/100011
- 93 Shchebetenko, S. (2017). Reflexive characteristic
  adaptations explain sex differences in the big five: but not in
  neuroticism. *Personality and Individual Differences, 111*,
  153-156. doi:10.1016/j.paid.2017.02.013

Giving Directions and Nagging

- 96 Ahn, J. N., Haines, E. L., & Mason, M. F. (2017). Gender
  stereotypes and the coordination of mnemonic work within
  heterosexual couples: romantic partners manage their daily
  to-dos. *Sex Roles, 77*(7-8), 435-452. doi:10.1007/s11199-
  017-0743-1

- 97 Kovac, K. (2018, April). Dr. Terri Orbuch reveals the secrets to happy relationships in the workplace and beyond. *Oakland Post.* https://oaklandpostonline.com/22392/campus/dr-terri-orbuch-reveals-the-secrets-to-happy-relationships-in-the-workplace-and-beyond/

Relationship Building

- 98 Gottman, J. M., & Silver, N. (2015). *The seven principles for making marriage work: a practical guide from the country's foremost relationship expert.* Harmony Books.

Listening

- 103 Doell, F (2003). "Partners' listening styles and relationship satisfaction: listening to understand vs. listening to respond." Graduate thesis. The University of Toronto Psychology Dept.

Humor

- 104 Bressler, E. R., Martin, R. A., & Balshine, S. (2006). Production and appreciation of humor as sexually selected traits. *Evolution and Human Behavior, 27*(2), 121-130. doi:10.1016/j.evolhumbehav.2005.09.001
- 106 Lampert, M. D., & Ervin-Tripp, S. M. (2006). Risky laughter: teasing and self-directed joking among male and female friends. *Journal of Pragmatics, 38*(1), 51-72. doi:10.1016/j.pragma.2005.06.004

Team Dynamic

- 112 Norman, L. (2016). Is there a need for coaches to be more gender responsive? a review of the evidence. *International Sport Coaching Journal, 3*(2), 192-196. doi:10.1123/iscj.2016-0032

Made in the USA
Coppell, TX
14 October 2021